TAKE A GIRL
LIKE ME

TAKE A GIRL LIKE ME

Amy Bohan

with Jordan Paramor

Beautiful
Books

Beautiful Books Limited
36-38 Glasshouse Street
London W1B 5DL

www.beautiful-books.co.uk

ISBN 9781905636488

9 8 7 6 5 4 3 2 1

This is a true story. Some of the names of individuals have
been changed.

A catalogue reference for this book is available
from the British Library.

Cover design by Ian Pickard.
Typesetting by Ellipsis Books Limited, Glasgow.
Printed in Great Britain by CPI Mackays, Chatham ME5 8TD

To mum, dad and my brother
for never giving up on me. x

INTRODUCTION

When I look back on everything that's happened to me over the last ten years I find it hard to believe that I haven't gone totally crazy. I know that everyone goes through a lot in their lives and I'm not one to feel sorry for myself, but I have had to deal with a lot over the last ten years or so and it's taken everything in me to pick myself up time after time. I've been beaten up, raped, been splashed on the front pages of tabloid newspapers, became a drug addict, ruined my modelling career and been so low that I honestly wondered how I would pick myself up again. In fact, a few times I decided that I didn't even want to try and I attempted to overdose just to try and escape the pain of everything.

Every day is still a struggle for me. Sometimes I can't even get myself out of bed in the mornings because my depression is so bad. I have to lie there for ages willing myself to get up and face another day and telling myself that things will get better. I'm lucky that I've got such a close family and some really good friends around me because without them I don't know how I would have survived.

I've learnt so much along the way and I'm doing my best to use all the negative things that have happened to build a better future for myself. I refuse to let my past become my future. What's done is done. All I can do is make sure I learn and move on.

When I was a kid I always dreamed that a knight in shining armour would come along and sweep me off my feet and whisk me off into the sunset. It's a cliché, but it's true. But if he came along now, I'd tell him to get back on his horse and ride away because honestly, I don't need rescuing. I'm strong and independent, and with each day that goes by I'm getting stronger. Depression is an ongoing battle for me, but it's one that I'm determined to win.

It's so strange to think that I went from being a normal girl next door to being on the front page of national newspapers for all the wrong reasons. I know that in part some of what's happened to me over the years has been my fault, but hopefully as you read this book you'll understand why I did the things I did and how I ended up having it all, only to lose it again.

Chapter 1

BABY STEPS

It's fair to say I had a very nice but pretty unremarkable childhood. I grew up in a lovely four-bedroom home in Mumbles in Wales with my younger brother and my parents. My mum worked as a nurse and my dad ran a travel company and the house was always immaculate. Mum was really house proud but it was a constant battle for her as we always had Labradors that used to shed their fur everywhere. She was always running around with the vacuum making sure that everything looked nice just in case people popped by.

I was quite a naughty child, but only in the way that other kids are. When I was about four I decided that I wanted my mum and dad's car to be yellow instead of the boring blue that it was. I got some squeezy yellow paint and a paintbrush and I started covering the bottom bits that I could reach. My parents were both in bed but when they got up they found me walking around the house covered in paint, and my mum's well-maintained carpets had little yellow footprints all over them. They managed to wash the paint off the car no problem, but it never did come out of the carpets properly. I wasn't very popular for a while!

I mainly hung around with kids in the area and I was always doing things after school, so I was always busy. I started doing ballet lessons when I was five, but I was asked to leave when I was six because I was far more interested in messing around than learning plies. My idea of sun wasn't wearing a tutu, it was running up and down the garden while my grandma timed me, or challenging my brother to climb the tallest tree we could find. I wasn't exactly graceful but I didn't mind. I was quite tough and I liked knowing that I could stand up for myself.

I wish I could say that my early childhood was more exciting but actually until the age of twelve everything was very normal and I was a really happy little girl. It was when I went to secondary school that things changed a bit. I had never really thought about whether I was pretty or not, but that soon changed. I had buck teeth and while all the other girls in my year were developing, I still had the body of a ten-year-old. I had no boobs to speak of but most of the girls in my class were already wearing bras. The boys used to do the 'bra test' where they used to sneak up behind and run their finger down your back so they could find out if you were wearing one or not. I didn't even own one so every time it was my turn to be tested I became a figure of fun. It wasn't like I was in the least bit interested in boys at that time – to me they were still just friends that I went on bike rides with or played British bulldog – but I did want to be accepted by the girls.

My limbs were also too long for my body and I was quite tall so people always used to call me 'Daddy Longlegs' and take the mickey out of me when we were playing sports – me in these tiny shorts. Someone once said that I looked like Bambi on stilts or like I had a couple of Mini Milks sticking out from under my skirts, both of which were fair comparisons. I didn't mind that so much because everyone gets called names at some point during their school days, but over the next couple of years the teasing got increasingly bad and eventually it turned into bullying. I started to hate school more and more knowing that as soon as I got there someone would start being nasty to me, and it got to the point where I would literally have to drag myself out of bed and put my uniform on.

I started to come home in tears every night and my school work started to suffer. My grades dipped hugely, mainly because I could never concentrate in my classes knowing full well that as soon as the next break came, I would spend the whole time being laughed at. There were also a couple of girls who would pass notes around about me saying mean things about how I looked like a boy and no one would ever fancy me. I had always been quite strong but it was relentless and it started to make me lose confidence in myself.

My school reports always said the same: 'Amy's a nice girl but she's really disruptive', and I think that was because I was so unhappy. I just didn't want to be at school in any way, shape or form. I did have some friends I could talk to but I felt like a real loser because I was being picked on so I tried to hide my feelings. And some people that I considered to be friends started to join in the bullying too, which hurt even more. I guess no one ever wants to hang around with someone who is a figure of fun in case they turn into one too. It's almost like being a geek by association.

I think as well as looking young for my age, another part of the problem was that while the so-called 'cool' girls were going out and getting drunk and getting off with boys, I started to get heavily into athletics, which they all found a bit weird. But for me running provided the perfect escape. If I was ever upset or down I'd put on my tracksuit and go for a run – it would clear my head and remind me that I had goals and aims and a real purpose in life.

I discovered my love for athletics by complete

coincidence. In fact if anything, athletics discovered me. When I was about 12 my PE teacher told me that I had to take part in a cross-country race against some other local schools. It sounded like a complete nightmare because I didn't have a clue if I'd be able to do it and I didn't want to get laughed at again, but I ended up winning the race. I was on such a high afterwards that I immediately wanted to go back and do it all again. I remember my mum coming to watch and being so proud that I'd won, but also really embarrassed because I was wearing a pair of cut off denim shorts and a really cool t-shirt. Hardly the usual cross country attire.

After that race I ran whenever I could and took part in loads of local competitions. It became my main hobby and it felt so good to have something I was good at, at long last. A short while afterwards a guy called John Griffiths came along to watch one of the races I was taking part in where several schools were competing against each other. Again, I won the race and afterwards he came up and asked me if I wanted to go and train with the Swansea Harriers Athletics Club. It was well known locally and had a really good reputation so I jumped at the chance. I found a good use for my Bambi legs.

Joining the Harriers was weird because I had never even thought about being sporty, but looking back I guess I was always a bit of a tomboy in some ways. I'd always done stuff like build tree houses with my younger brother, Michael, and all those timed runs in my back garden had clearly paid off. The fact that I wasn't very girlie and hadn't started to wear make-up meant that I didn't mind running through muddy puddles and getting soaked in the rain. It really didn't bother me, and I liked getting the chance to break free from everything and just be myself, no matter how dirty that meant I ended up.

The bullying at school continued for quite a while. The same group of girls would follow me every day and call me names. They had got bored of taking the mickey out of my legs so they started on my teeth and they'd call me gerbil and hamster teeth. It was so pathetic and I know it's not exactly life threatening, but it started to really get to me. It may have been silly but it was also relentless. Thankfully the bullying had never got really physical, but one day this huge girl called Carol picked me up and threw me against a wall. It wasn't for any particular reason; it was just because she could. She was a very big girl and very powerful and I'll never forget the fear I felt when she came looming towards me with a look of determination on her face. If anything I think I got off quite lightly. It could have been a lot worse – I'd seen her do worse to other people.

Needless to say it made me very nervous about going to school and I think when you're bullied, you always think that in some way it's your own fault because you're unlikable. It made me feel very lonely and isolated from other people, especially as most of my 'friends' had distanced themselves from me the worse the bullying got.

I did have one really good friend, Louisa, who was always really naughty. I remember her locking the RE teacher in a cupboard once during a class when she went in there to get something, and another time we decided that we would walk to school but we messed around so much on the way that we didn't arrive until it was time to go home again and we got a letter sent home accusing us of bunking off. But at least we'd *tried* to get there! But that was really the extent of my naughtiness at school. I was pretty unremarkable and will probably only ever be remembered because of sport.

Being a part of the running club really helped me to stay positive and I made some good friends there. My mum also bought me a white horse called Misty so that I had something else to concentrate my energy on. I think she thought horse riding would be another good way for me to make new friends away from school, and she was right. I got on really well with the girls at the stables because they were like me and they thought there was more to life than lip gloss and boy bands. Riding also provided me with a way to escape, and it taught me discipline. I had to go and muck Misty out before and after school and on weekends and if I missed a session there was no one else there to do it for me so I had no choice. So while my peers were out drinking cider on street corners I was busy with the horses and was very well behaved. Maybe too well behaved? Maybe that's part of the reason I went so spectacularly off the rails later on in life?

Even though I made some friends outside school I was still very unhappy when I was at school, and the bullying showed no signs of stopping. Eventually my parents decided that it would be best if they sent me to a private school where I could have a fresh start. They found a private school that was near our house. I was really excited about going somewhere new but a few days after I joined I realised that it was full of rich kids and I soon started to feel a bit out of place there as well. All the girls there had designer clothes and went on expensive holidays and again, I didn't feel like I fitted in. I remember going home to my mum crying and saying that I would never fit in anywhere.

After my initial panic, within a few weeks things started to get better. I think because it was a much smaller school than the last one I'd been to, in some ways I found it easier to handle as I didn't feel so lost. They were much more open to the idea of girls doing a lot of sport and because I excelled in athletics that made me stand out, which in turn made me feel more confident. Hardly a day went past when the headmaster didn't walk into assembly and mention my name for doing something well in athletics or winning some race or another. Because of that I was respected by my schoolmates and I started to feel more accepted. Within six months my life had improved no end. The bitchy girls couldn't get to me any more and I soon made some good friends. At least I was happy and settled.

Even as I got older I wasn't really one for going out in the evenings or going shopping at weekends with mates because my life was all about running. I trained with the Harriers on Tuesday and Thursday nights, and then again on Saturday mornings. I would also train by myself most other evenings so it didn't leave a lot of time for much else. That kind of suited me though. I still saw myself as a tomboy and I don't think I even owned a dress to go out in at that time even if I had wanted to.

Chapter 2

KEEP ON RUNNING

The Harriers training sessions were always really competitive, but I loved it. And the better I did, the happier I was. I represented Swansea, West Glamorgan, then Wales in competitions over a period of about seven years, and I was always in the top five without fail. My family were really proud of me and always came along to watch me in competitions, and it was always assumed that running would be my career. I had no idea what else I wanted to do. It was really all I enjoyed.

I felt such a sense of freedom when I was running and I loved it when we got to travel around. I used to take part in the British Schools International Cross Country races in Durham, Irvine, Chepstow and Dublin. I also took part in the British Schools International track and field, usually doing 3000 metres. I especially used to love competing against the English teams for some reason. They were always so proper and had really good manners, whereas we were a bit more rowdy. Whenever we had after match dinners we'd try and start a food fight with them but they were too well behaved, so we'd sit there throwing carrots and stuff at them. That was about as wild as my life was back then.

When I was 17 I was running in a race in Neath and I got scouted by another trainer called Jeremy. He came up to me after the race and asked if I would join his training group, Team US. He was a British 400 metres coach and had trained people for the Olympics, so it was a definite step up. Daniel Caines, who went on to win a world indoor medal, was in my group, and it was a lot more structured than the Harriers had been, meaning that there was a lot more pressure on us. There was no chatting while we were warming up or messing around while we were waiting to run. You didn't speak, you focused – and it was like taking things to a totally different level.

My dream was always to go to the Commonwealth Games and compete. I was always realistic about what I could achieve and I never thought that I would go all the way to the Olympics, win a gold medal and be a world champion. I always trained much better than I raced for some reason, which was annoying as it meant that so much was expected of me but I couldn't always follow through with it. Despite that I did think that making the Welsh team for the Commonwealth Games was well within my reach. My aim was to go to Sydney in 2006 to compete, but needless to say due to all of the circumstances you'll read about in this book, I never did make it there.

I guess in some ways I did miss out on a lot during my teenage years and they were probably very different from a lot of other people's. But I achieved a lot while other people were drinking cheap cider at youth clubs, so I don't regret the choices I made back then. I think if I'd stayed at my first school my life would have felt very different because I may have succumbed to the pressure of going out, but at the private school people were much more individual and everyone accepted people the way they were.

The fact that I was so focused on athletics definitely affected my relationship with boys because I just wasn't interested. I didn't want to get into anything that would take my attention away from the athletics, and as a result I didn't have my first boyfriend until I was in my late teens.

It's weird because I always had so many more male friends than female friends because of my involvement in sport, so you would think it would have been easy to find a boyfriend, but it just didn't happen. All my male friends saw me as one of the boys so I don't think they ever considered me to be girlfriend material. I was just Amy: a good laugh and their good mate. My hair was usually short and scruffy and I spent most of my time wearing track-suits and trainers. I also never wore make-up and barely even owned any apart from what my mum would buy me for Christmas, so I wasn't what you'd call super-feminine. Most of the time I didn't even think about what I looked like. It wasn't exactly my number one priority and I was never one of the people fighting for the mirror in the toilets at lunch-time. My classmates would be worrying about what colour to dye their hair or which heels they should buy for that weekend, and I was preoccupied with thoughts of getting my running times down.

I guess you could say I was a plain Jane. In fact, some of the other girls who wanted to be models at school used to make fun of me and say, 'You could be a model Amy,' and then laugh, and I'd shrug it off and laugh along with them thinking 'never in a million years would I do something like that anyway'.

Back then I would much rather read a rugby mag-azine than Cosmopolitan so I didn't really fit in with other girls, and I always felt a lot more comfortable with my male friends. They were far less judgmental of me and I found them more interesting to be around. I became good friends with one guy in particular, Bean, and he's still one of my best mates today. So when it came to lunchtimes and hanging out after school I would always be with him.

I know that some of the other girls thought I was strange not wanting to hang out with them, and some of them could be a bit bitchy because I think they felt threatened that I was different to them. I also don't think it helped that a lot of them fancied Bean so they were envious of me hanging out with him all the time. I was also good friends with the rugby player Jonny Vaughton, who was drop dead gorgeous even then with these amazing piercing eyes, so that didn't make me terribly popular either! Literally all of the girls fancied him, but as stunning as he was, I didn't. We were just friends and that was enough for me.

As I got older I started to experiment with going out a bit more but I still really limited it. I may have gone out on a Saturday and got drunk with some friends every now and again, but then it would be another six weeks before I went out again. I didn't want alcohol in my system or to put on weight. Not because I was worried about how I looked, but because it would affect my performance.

It's funny because I never even gave a thought to my weight, but it did seem to be an issue for other people. One of my teachers even called my mum up once and told her she thought I had an eating disorder because I was so slim. I was probably a size six to eight and I didn't have boobs, and a bum and thighs like other girls my age, but there was certainly nothing wrong with me. When you're running as much as I was you're bound to be slim, but there was never any question of me being unwell. Had other people not made a big deal of it I would never have really given my body shape a second thought, but it's funny how what you look like affects other people. It was something that was mentioned to me a lot and I always thought it was strange that anyone else would care how much I weighed.

It was only when I started doing my A-levels that I felt a bit more pressure to be a bit more sociable and I started to go out every couple of weeks or so, but only if there was a reason like it was someone's birthday or something. I was just as happy staying at home with my family and watching TV. It's hard to believe that I thought pubs and clubs were boring considering how much of a party monster I turned into.

I studied my A-Levels at Olchfa College, quite near my home. I was doing English Language, English Literature, PE and Psychology A-Levels, but I soon realised that it wasn't for me – I had got a bit sick of school life. I did well in my CGSE's and got ten B's and C's, but I felt like I needed some time out from the relentlessness of lessons so I decided to drop out. My parents weren't happy but I explained to them that it was either that, or I kept skipping lessons and got thrown out anyway. I'd made my mind up. I got a job in a local clothes shop for a while just to earn some money and I carried on my sports training. But I soon discovered that working full time was much harder than going to college so the next year I decided to enroll all over again. I think because I knew if I didn't make a go of it this time I would end up back working in a shop again, that made me knuckle down and dedicate myself. I was a lot happier in college the second time around generally. I met some nice people, I felt better equipped to deal with the work and I felt pretty happy.

One thing I had been dreaming about doing for a really long time was learning to drive. Sadly, I wasn't a natural. My parents paid for me to have lessons and I lost count of the amount of times I nearly crashed.

My first driving instructor was a guy called Richard who was a member of some bizarre religious cult. He and I didn't really see eye to eye, and he annoyed me with his constant talk of religion and how I was 'sinning' for various reasons. I was a pedal to the metal kind of girl, and he was forever slamming his foot on the brake on his side. I suspect I drove him a bit crazy, if you'll pardon the pun. It wasn't like I wasn't trying to drive, I just couldn't get the hang of it at all and I thought that if I went fast it would look like I knew what I was doing. After a while he refused to teach me any more saying he didn't really appreciate my need for speed. He knew my Nan and he told her that I was a hooligan and could no longer deal with me. I thought that was a bit over the top, but then I thought back to the time I went round a roundabout the wrong way, and the numerous times I'd stuck my fingers up at other drivers when they'd beeped me and decided that maybe he had a point. I don't think he was the ideal person to teach me.

I got another instructor who was also Carmarthen Harriers Athletics Coach who I had a lot more in common with. He could see how nervous I was and why I was zooming around, so we went back to basics and he taught me all over again. After two weeks of lessons with him I was doing three point turns and reverse parking no problem, and I felt more comfortable with driving than I ever had.

After months and months of lessons, I was so happy when I passed my driving test on my fifth attempt. It meant that I had total and utter freedom and I couldn't wait to be able to drive myself to training and to see my friends. My parents bought me a brand new purple Citroen AX and I had never been so proud of anything in my life. I filled it up with all my stuff and I had a massive smile on my face the first time I pulled out of our driveway with no one sitting beside me.

The first thing I did was go and pick my friend Bean up from college and then drop him home again, just because I could. I felt so proud pulling up outside the college and waited there for ages so lots of people saw me. I was on a roll so I called another friend of mine called Amy and asked her if she fancied going for a drive. I thought I was really cool driving around all over the place and we zoomed all around the cliffs of Mumbles for about three hours. When it was time to take Amy home I decided that it would be a good idea to do a three-point turn in the middle of the road, only it didn't go exactly as planned I nearly drove us over the edge of a cliff. We were screaming our heads off and how I managed to stop the car sliding off I'll never know, but I rammed it straight in reverse and we didn't stop screaming until we were safely on flat ground again.

Amy and I decided to go and visit Bean so we could have a cup of tea and calm down. But as I drove up the hill towards his house I went straight into the back of another car. A police car. I wasn't even going fast – in fact, I must have been going about ten miles an hour – I just wasn't looking where I was going. There was a gorgeous guy over the other side of the road and I had been too busy checking him out to concentrate on what was in front of me.

I was so embarrassed and I'll never forget the policeman storming out of his car and spending absolutely ages inspecting the back for damages. He made a real drama out of it but there were literally a few scratches; there wasn't even a bump. It was so ridiculous, but what was even more ridiculous was that he went on to claim he had whiplash, and even took time off work because of it. Thankfully I didn't get arrested or anything, I just got a warning, but all in all my first day out on the open road wasn't a very successful one.

I was really worried about was what my mum would say about my little collision, so I got Amy's mum to call her and explain what had happened. Thankfully she was really cool about it once she knew that no one had been injured, and she even laughed a little when she found out that it was a policeman I'd gone into. She didn't find my next crash quite as funny though . . .

About a week later I was coming home from a nightclub and I was dropping friends home. I had got my confidence back after my disastrous first driving day and I was bombing it along these little roads near my house. I had lived there all my life and I knew the roads like the back of my hand so I was convinced that I'd be fine. I hadn't drunk a drop of alcohol, but as we went around this corner the road veered off to the right, but I carried on going straight and we crashed straight into this lamppost. I think I must have been in shock because I turned the engine back on and tried to reverse the car out so I could carry on, but there was loads of smoke coming out of the engine. Jonny was busy trying to pick his kebab off the floor so I got out to inspect the damage and he just looked at me and said, 'Your mum will freak.' We sat in the car for a couple of hours deciding what to do and eventually I called my mum. She was calm about it but I could tell she was alarmed and obviously very concerned about my driving skills. She wasn't the only one.

I decided to take things a bit easier after that. My beautiful, brand new car was a total write off and I was so upset. As soon as I saved up enough money to buy myself another car, a Vauxhall Corsa, I took things a whole lot easier. There was no more zooming around country lanes or three point turns on unsafe roads, and I am proud to say that I haven't had an accident since. A bad *incident*, yes – which we'll come to later on in the book – but no accidents.

Sixth-form college was all about me growing up. I started to grow my hair a bit longer and I even started wearing make up when I went out. I remember buying my first pair of high heels, which I found hysterical. I was so tall anyway and they made my legs look about a mile long. I felt like how I imagine a boy would feel if they were to try on some high shoes. My friend Amy was laughing her head off as she watched me try and walk around the shop without falling over, but I decided that it was time for me to be a bit more ladylike so I bought them anyway.

I practiced wearing them at home for a bit before

I plucked up the courage to wear them out, but when I did all my male friends kept telling me how good I looked so that gave me the confidence to wear them again. I think they were all really shocked to see my out of flat shoes or trainers, but I found that I quite liked the attention.

I started going out a lot more and although I was still training regularly, I found other interests apart from running. It was as if my teens were finally catching up with me and I wanted to go out and have fun. I had quite a big group of friends by then and we all used to go into town on Saturday nights together. I still didn't drink very often so I was usually the one who would drive everyone home, but I didn't mind a bit. I didn't mind alcohol but I could have just as good a time without it.

Having done pretty well in my A-levels I decided to go on and do an HND in sports and exercise science at Swansea College. As far as I was concerned I was going to have a career in athletics, full stop, but I knew that I also needed something to fall back on should I ever get injured or anything. I knew that I would always want to be involved in sports in some way because it was the thing I had the most passion for, so my aim was to become a qualified sports masseuse.

I started doing work experience at Bridgend Ravens Rugby Club helping out as a sport coach. When I turned up at the WRU barn for my first day at work I was slightly nervous as the day's training had already begun. I was taken over to meet all the guys and I remember thinking that for big beefy rugby guys, they were surprisingly sweet and friendly. The boys were doing a speed, quickness and agility session and I recognised a few of the players and very quickly found my favourites. I noticed that Alfie trained extremely hard, harder than most – I heard he even trained after training in the gym at his home. I'd never seen someone do as much resistance training as Goose, and Lelo had a million dollar smile. Overall they were the nicest bunch of boys you'd ever want to meet.

After a couple of weeks of being there I went out for a night with some of the guys, including a South African guy we used to call Flash. He was constantly in trouble but that night I went out with him he was really well behaved and hardly drank a thing.

When I turned up for work the next day I was in the office when someone with too much time on their hands rang to complain because Flash had been seen out in the town. He said that Flash and another player were causing trouble in the club we'd been in, which was complete crap. I told him so and put the phone down on him. I think after that I was considered to be a proper part of the team. I ended up staying there for almost a year helping out and I'm still really good friends with some of the players now.

I loved my time there and I some of my happiest memories are of me working there. However, it was also while I was doing my HND and working at Bridgend that I met the guy who was to become my first boyfriend. And my life would change forever.

Chapter 3

RUNNING
IN HEELS

Until I bought that first pair of heels I never even really thought about guys fancying me that much. I assumed they would always just see me as a mate the way that all my male friends in the past had done. But all of a sudden some guys started telling me I was hot when we were out clubbing, and I was so shocked because I'd never seen myself as being at all pretty. I still felt like the same plain girl I had always been, but I suppose somewhere along the way I blossomed and being tall and slim was no longer such a bad thing.

All of the nice comments I got gave me a bit of a boost and I started to think about guys more as potential boyfriends than just mates. I had lots of male friends who played rugby and although all of the other girls really liked them, to me they had always been people I hung out with. But all that changed when I met a guy while I was down at

Merthyr Mawr sand dunes in Bridgend one day. I was doing my athletics training and he was doing rugby training. He had a coach with him that I knew, and for some reason the rest of my team hadn't turned up for practice, so the coach asked if I wanted to train with them.

The rugby player was really sweet and introduced himself to me as Gavin, but although I didn't let on, I already knew who he was as he was making quite a name for himself as a rugby player for Wales. I had a read a few things in the local paper about this guy called Gavin Henson who was being touted as the next big thing. I didn't think much of the fact that he was well known and I wasn't in the least bit impressed. I had run for Wales so I didn't think of what he was doing as any different to what I had achieved.

Gavin was really handsome even back then, and he had this air of confidence about him, but he also seemed quite shy in a way. I'll never forget the first time I saw him smile. My first thought was 'He's really cute,' and my second was 'Wow, he's got really, really white teeth.' I think his glowing helped to show them off!

From the moment we started chatting there was definitely something between us; something I had never felt with a guy before. I didn't want this guy to be just my friend. I thought he was really sexy and for the first time in my life I found myself flirting. I had never really flirted properly before so it was a whole new world for me, and looking back I was probably the worst flirt in the world. If Gavin thought the same he didn't show it. He was happy to stay and talk to me for ages after training finished and I got the feeling he was flirting with me too . . .

After that first meeting I kept bumping into Gavin around Swansea. We'd always check to see that the other one would be training the following Saturday so we could see each other. It was obvious that we both liked each other but neither of us was brave enough to say anything so we just used to tease each other and do silly, flirty things.

We always spent time talking to each other at training and we made any excuse we could to spend time together. We used to spend a long time training on the sand dunes together because they were one of the quietest areas and we could spend as long as we liked chatting to each other.

A few months passed and I began to think that maybe I had read the signs wrong and Gavin did see me as just a friend after all.

I didn't really know how these things worked but I was pretty sure that if he liked me he would have said something by now, or at least asked me out on a date. But then on my 20th birthday he finally made his feelings known.

I'd gone to the Walkabout Bar in town with all

of my friends. I was all dressed up and I'd made a real effort to look glamorous. It was the only time Gavin had ever seen me either not wearing jeans or a scruffy tracksuit, and I'll never forget the look on his face when he walked in and saw me. He marched straight up to me, smiled and said, 'You and me – later.' I giggled and he asked where I was going later, and when I turned up to a club called Envy afterwards he was there waiting for me. We both made it clear that we fancied each like mad and literally left straight away and went back to the hotel he was staying at nearby. He didn't live in Swansea so whenever he was there for training or a night out he would stay in hotels. It seems bizarre that I did that now as I would never go back and stay with a guy I didn't know very well at a hotel, but I was totally swept away with the romance of it all. I assumed that was what everyone did on first dates!

I didn't sleep with him that night but we had a great time and stayed up chatting most of the night. We had loads in common because of our love of sports and I found him so easy to talk to. Although we both liked each other as more than friends we had become friends first, which I think really helped. We really got each other and it wasn't how I imagined seeing someone would be. I assumed that once something romantic happened between two people you can't really be proper friends any more because you're always putting on a show and trying to impress each other, but we were very natural in each other's company.

After that night we started seeing quite a lot of each other and we'd hook up whenever we were out and about. We never arranged to meet as such, but we always knew where the other one would be. We'd usually meet up in the Walkabout or Time or Envy, have a few drinks and then go for a drive or back to Gavin's hotel. Neither of us ever talked about any kind of commitment or where the relationship was heading. We were just having fun and taking each date as it comes.

The first time I knew for sure that Gavin was properly into me was when he came looking for me one night. I used to go out every Monday night with my male friends from college to parties in the student union. Gavin had never been because he wasn't at the college, but it was open to people from outside if they had friends who went there. One evening I was having a few drinks with my mates in the union and he turned up. It was quite out of the way for him to get to, so he must have made a special effort, and as much as I tried to hide it, I was really excited.

As soon as he walked through the door I spotted him but I didn't go over and see him or anything. I decided that if he wanted to see me he would find me. All the girls knew who he was so they were flocking around him and hanging off every word he said. One girl even went up and saluted him and then slipped her phone number into his pocket. I just laughed because I knew that he couldn't stand girls like that, so they weren't doing themselves any favours.

He did eventually come and find me and pretended to be surprised that I was there, but he later admitted that he was on a mission to find me. We ended up leaving together and the look on the faces of all the girls was priceless. They may as well have gone up to him and asked him why the hell he was leaving with someone like me when they were basically offering themselves to him. They looked horrified. No one really knew that we'd been seeing each other so all my male friends were really surprised too, but I got quite a few 'well dones' from them.

In time I got used to the rugby groupies being around and it didn't make me feel insecure. I knew that at the end of the evening Gavin would be leaving with me. But it did get quite uncomfortable sometimes. If I was out for the night with him girls would flock around him giggling and pretending to know the ins and outs of rugby. I may as well have been invisible for all they cared; it was as if they didn't even notice I was there even though Gavin was blatantly with me. If we were sitting down somewhere girls would come and party at the end of the table in the hope of being noticed by him, or come up and offer to buy him drinks. They were totally shameless.

The funny thing was that I'd be there dressed in jeans and heels and usually one of Gavin's jumpers, and they'd be there with their boobs hanging out in these tiny dresses but he didn't give them a second look. He always said that he liked girls who were down to earth and natural, and with my mainly make-up free face and hair tucked behind my ears you couldn't get much more natural than me.

Gavin and I used to laugh a lot together and we were always doing stupid things. Sometimes I used to think we were more like brother and sister than girlfriend and boyfriend because we didn't care what we did or said in front of each other. I remember this one time in particular we were staying back at Gavin's hotel. We were just about to go to sleep and he announced that he'd bought an Elvis costume that day. Not for any reason, just because he fancied owning one. He asked if I wanted to see it and as soon as I said yes he leapt out of bed, whipped the costume out of the bag and put the whole lot on; the white trouser suit, the wig and the gold Vegas-style glasses. His mate was in the room next door and he came and asked us to be quiet, so Gavin suggested that we both went and sat in the corridor and carried on talking out there. We'd had a few drinks so it seemed like a good idea at the time. It was about two in the morning so there were loads of people coming back from nights out and there was Gavin sat there in this Elvis costume. We were both singing Elvis songs to all the people who were coming back and Gavin turned round to me and said, 'Do you think they recognise me?' and I laughed and said, 'Not even your mum would recognise you in that outfit!'

As much as Gavin and I liked each other's company and had a great time together it's not like we were in love. We were like friends with benefits, in a way. Even though neither of us slept with other people while we were going out with each other our relationship always remained very light hearted.

I'll never forget the time a friend of mine from college told me he'd seen Gavin and I out and about over the weekend. He said he'd seen the pair of us staggering up the main high street and he'd turned to his girlfriend and said, 'That girl is an international athlete and that guy is an international rugby player, and look at the state of them.' Gavin laughed so much when I told him. It made me realise that all my years of sports had paid off. While other girls had been going out clubbing for years and having fun I had been spending my evenings pounding grass and doing star jumps. But here I was with the guy that every girl wanted to be with, and he liked me because I was as passionate about sport as he was. We were such a good match.

We carried in seeing each other for a few months, but after all the fun we'd had things came to a horrible end, suddenly one night. We'd all been out to a club and I remember Gavin letting me drive his Audi TT back to his friend's house because he'd been drinking. I was so excited about it, I was still a secret speed freak. We got to his mate's house and they had told us to let ourselves in with the key that was hidden under a bin bag. We were there for ages throwing all these bin bags around and trying to locate the key but it was nowhere to be found. In the end Gavin, who was quite drunk, decided to ring on the doorbell on the off chance that someone was in. After a lot of moving around this old woman answered the door and shouted, 'What do you want? You're that rugby player, aren't you?' We'd gone to the wrong house. Gavin drunkenly asked if his mates lived there and she shouted a firm 'No,' and slammed the door in our faces. She wasn't happy. But it was two o'clock, so who can blame her?

Eventually we found Gavin's friend's house – and the key – and let ourselves in, but as I had training early the next day at about three o' clock I told Gavin I was going home. He was a bit annoyed as he thought I going to be staying the night with him, but once I explained he said he understood and offered to walk me to get a cab. He and his friends were all drinking and having a good time so I told him I'd be fine on my own. He also had training the next day too and he needed to get some sleep, and besides, it wasn't far to walk to get a taxi. I kissed him goodbye and started to walk back into town. There were always loads of cabs on the main high street and it was only about ten minutes away.

I had always felt like I could look after myself no problem and had walked around in the dark on my own before. Plus I was stone cold sober so it wasn't as if someone could easily take advantage of me. I'm 5' 10" and although I was slim I was also quite muscular from all the training I did. In fact, I could lift a 40kg bench press and lift 60kg no problem, so I didn't really give it a second thought when I was walking down a dark street all alone. Crazy, really.

It was November so it was really cold outside and I was walking fast, and as I made my way down a street called Henrietta Street I saw this guy lingering behind a wall wearing a grey hoodie and black trousers. I could feel him watching me as I walked past and as I carried on walking quickly I could tell that he was following me. It was just this weird instinct I had that I was in real danger and that something bad was going to happen. I started to panic but I took deep breaths and tried to stay as calm as I could. I thought if I appeared afraid I would look weaker.

I started to feel increasingly scared as I heard him speed up and get nearer to me. I didn't dare look around and I knew there was no point in trying to get away. I had stress fractures in my feet so it was more difficult for me run than usual, so I felt like I had no choice – I turned around to confront him. The next thing I knew I had been pushed backwards and thrown on top of this huge pile of rubbish. I tried so hard to get away but he was too strong for me and he climbed on top of me and held me down. At no point did I think I was going to die, but I was still absolutely terrified. I just wanted him to do whatever he was going to do and for it to be over.

I lay on the ground with my eyes wide open staring at the sky. As much as I tried to scream, nothing would come out of my mouth. It was like when you go on a rollercoaster at the fair and you're petrified, but when you open your mouth you can't make any noise. I remember saying, 'Mum help me' but he told me to shut up and put his hand over my mouth.

He didn't speak to me at all apart from that, he just growled every now and again. I don't want to go into too many details as I don't think it's necessary but I will say that as he held me down he sexually assaulted me before spitting in my face. He then got up and walked off, leaving me lying there. He was so arrogant that he didn't even bother to run away, he just walked up the street as if it were the most normal thing in the world.

I lay there feeling numb, cold and shocked. I just wanted to be at home, safe in my bed. I managed to stand up and get myself together. I was in pain from where he'd thrown me down and used force on me, but in my mind the only thing to do was carry on walking into town and try and get a taxi to safety.

I must have looked like I was in a bit of a state because these guys approached me to ask if I was okay. I started screaming at the top of my voice and telling them not to touch me and they backed away from me, horrified. A few minutes up the road I came across a pizza take away place and I called my friend Alan, who is a police officer, and told him what had happened. I was crying and I kept asking him over and over what I was going to do. In my state I got it into my head that my parents were going to be angry with me for being so stupid and putting myself in danger. I thought it was all my fault.

Alan called the police for me and they came to collect me and took me to the station. They were asking me all these questions but all I could re-member were these white bin bags lying against a white wall. I told them about the party and about Gavin offering to walk me to a taxi and as much as they tried to be sympathetic, I could tell they thought I had been very foolish to turn down his offer.

They took me out in a squad car to see if I could pinpoint the place where the attack had happened, but it was so dark that I could barely see and there was no way I was going to find it. All the houses looked the same and as we drove everything became a bit of a blur.

The police kept saying that they were going to go and wake Gavin up and get his side of the story. I could tell that they only wanted to go and see him because of who he was. I could hear them all discussing it outside the room saying, 'Who's going to go up Gavin Henson's house then?' like it was some kind of prize. I was thinking, 'What would be the point in doing that?' It wasn't like he could tell them anything, and I thought it would have been really unfair to wake him up. It was about five o'clock in the morning by that point.

I was really firm with them and told them I wanted them to leave Gavin alone, but of course they didn't. They stormed straight over there and started asking him questions about whether I'd been drinking and what time I left. They could easily have left it until the next day but they clearly wanted to be able to be the ones to say that they'd questioned him.

Needless to say Gavin was really upset by what they told him. After the police left he ended up having a massive row with his friends about it all and he went and slept in his car. I think a couple of them had a go at him and said he should have made sure I got into a taxi safely, but it had been my decision. I know that in that kind of situation where you're hurt and in pain you're supposed to put yourself first and worry about how you'll cope, but all I could think about was Gavin. I felt so bad for him getting hassle from other people. It wasn't his fault in any way, and yet he was being made to feel like he was to blame.

Once I found out that the police had been to see Gavin I made the police take me home immediately. I was so angry I wanted to be as far away from there as possible. I felt so confused and I needed the comfort and safety of my home.

My parents were away on holiday and my brother was away at University so there was no one in the house when I got in. I shut all the security gates, locked all the doors and lay on my bed and cried for ages. I had a bath followed by a shower and I scrubbed myself until it hurt. I went downstairs and started pacing around the living room. I didn't know what else I could do to make myself feel better. And then I spotted the drinks cabinet. I opened a bottle of vodka and started drinking it straight down. I sat on the sofa and carried on glugging and before I knew it I'd finished the bottle. I can't say it made me feel better but it did help to numb me slightly and for the first time in hours I stopped crying. I went looking for more alcohol but as my parents aren't big drinkers there wasn't a lot to choose from so I grabbed a bottle of rum, which I later discovered was cooking rum. It tasted awful but I didn't care about that. It was numbing all of my feelings, and that was what I needed most.

Gavin was ringing and ringing me on my mobile but I didn't take any of his calls. I just didn't know what to say to him. I wanted to tell him that I didn't blame him but I felt like everything would come out wrong, so I kept dropping his calls. I stayed awake for what was left of the night and around ten in the morning my Auntie Jacquie called to check my brother and I were okay without my parents. I must have sounded like I was in a bit of a state, and probably very drunk. She asked me if I was okay and I broke down and started screaming and crying down the phone that I'd been attacked. She got straight into her car and drove all the way up from Weymouth to be with me. She's got a daughter called Tilly who was 17 at the time and she kept ringing me every 15 minutes until my auntie arrived to make sure I was okay. I was still drinking and I think they were worried that I was going to pass out or do something stupid.

I was so relieved when my auntie arrived. I hadn't been able to bring myself to tell any of my friends what had happened so I'd had no one to comfort me. But even when I saw my auntie I still couldn't bring myself to reveal the full details of what had gone on. I couldn't talk about it without crying and it brought it all back. She wanted to call my parents and tell them but they were due back the next day and I didn't want to ruin their holiday. Also, I didn't want them finding out about something like that on the phone and then getting in a state because they were too far away to do anything.

My auntie stayed with me until my parents got home, and as soon as they walked through the door I felt safe again. My mum hugged me for ages but my dad didn't really know what to say or do. I think it's hard for dads to imagine their daughter having to go through something like that. I think more than anything he felt massive anger about everything. He didn't really say anything for the first few hours he was home, and then he turned and said to me, 'Do you want to go for a run?' Five minutes later I went upstairs and came down in my tracksuit and we went out running together for about two hours. I guess that was my dad's way of bonding with me, as he didn't know any other way to reach out to me.

My brother was furious when he found out what had happened and offered to come home straight away. Obviously he was full of ideas about going out and finding the guy, but I told him to stay put. He couldn't do anything if he came home and there was such a downbeat atmosphere in the house that I wanted us to try and move on from it as quickly as possible.

Sadly not all of my family were quite as understanding as my parents and brother. One older relative turned around and said to me, 'Well what did you expect? Walking around on your own in the dark? It's a ridiculous thing to do.' Another relative said to me when she saw me, 'Oh, you look alright, no one will ever know.' That wasn't exactly what I needed to hear. Those two incidents made me feel worse than ever and like it had all been my fault.

Not surprisingly the attack affected me really badly and for ages afterwards it was all I could think about. I started to get really nervous around men, and because I didn't really tell anyone what had happened no one knew why I was acting so strangely. I think some of my male friends thought I was losing the plot a bit.

I remember one of my mates from college asking me why I didn't go to the common room any more, and I lied and said that I'd been really busy with some extra college projects I'd taken on. I daren't tell anyone the truth: that whenever I had spare time I would spend it driving up and down the road where the attack happened, over and over again hoping to see the guy so I could tell the police where he lived or hung out. My other plan was to follow him to wherever he lived and then send someone over there to sort him out. I was so angry I wasn't thinking straight. I wanted him to suffer like I had. Sometimes I would be driving around for hours staring at the faces of every man I passed. I wasn't even sure that I would recognise him as it had been so dark, but I felt like I would instinctively 'know' it was him. I wanted some justice and for him to pay for what he had done to me.

My moods become more and more erratic and I would cry at the smallest thing, so my mum suggested that I should go to a counsellor to try and work through what had happened. I flatly refused. I didn't see what use talking about it would do, it would just bring it all back up again. I decided that the answer was alcohol.

Even though I was feeling low I was determined to finish my HND course. I didn't want the attack to affect my entire future. So I was still going to college every day as normal, but every night I'd come home, lock myself in my room and drink vodka. It became like a routine and I stopped going out with other people completely. I cut myself off from my friends and I lived in my own little bubble of booze.

Gavin was always at the back of my mind but even though he'd tried to call me a couple more times, I still wasn't ready to speak to him. I don't think either of us could handle what had gone on and we avoided each other completely. I think we both needed time to ourselves to mull things over and let the dust settle.

When I was finally ready to see him I called and we arranged to meet up just around the corner from

St Helen's Rugby Club in Swansea. I felt like I at least needed to let him see that I was okay and make sure that he wasn't harbouring any guilt. My head was in a mess but there was no reason his needed to be. I was very nervous going along to meet him but I knew that we had to say goodbye properly and put an end to things once and for all. The minute I saw him I wanted to cry as I remembered all of the good times that we'd had together, but things were understandably very tense between us. There was no kiss or hug hello, and neither of us spoke for a good few minutes as we shuffled around looking everywhere but at each other.

Eventually I broke the silence. I had bought him a silver bracelet as a gift to say goodbye, and I gave it to him and thanked him for all the fun times we'd had together. I told him that I didn't blame him for anything and that none of it was his fault, but he still couldn't look at me. He just kept staring at the floor. We only stayed for ten minutes or so and it was clear that we both wanted to get away as quickly as possible so I said to him, 'Look, you've got your rugby to concentrate on and I've got athletics. Let's leave things for now and maybe hook up in 20 years time and swap medal stories.'

I tried to keep it as light-hearted as possible but I felt a couple of tears running down my cheeks. He had tears in his eyes as well and for the first time he looked at me and said, 'Your life is ruined. I hate myself for not walking you home.' I hugged him and told him I would be okay, then we both turned and walked in opposite directions and that was the end of our relationship.

It felt like the end of an era and it was sad saying goodbye to someone that I cared about so much. But I didn't cry or even feel that sad when I got in my car to drive home. I think because I was still so numb from the attack. It was as if I couldn't really feel much at all.

I saw Gavin out and about a few times afterwards and it was always very awkward. I don't think he told many of his friends what happened and someone else told me that he had said that we had split up because I did some horrible things, which made me feel really let down. I know it wasn't like we were about to rush off and get married but we did really care about each other and we'd had some really good times. I guess he just needed to give his friends some reason – any reason – for the split. He was so worried about his image and I always wondered if one of the reasons he went out with me was because I was quite well known in Swansea. It seemed to me that he was doing all he could to protect the image he had created for himself. Even back then he was obsessed with designer clothes and he was always meticulously dressed with a deep tan. It was his 'look'.

Gavin and I were just young and we didn't know

how to handle the attack so we both backed away
from each other. But it's a shame that it happened
the way it did as I think in any other circumstances
we would have stayed friends after we had split
up.

Chapter 4

A FEW STEPS
BACK...

I was doing my best to live my life day to day as normally as possible, but mentally things were getting worse and worse. I was barely sleeping because I was having nightmares and I began to wonder if things would ever get better. I was drinking just to get to sleep each night, and a few times I drank so much I woke up in my own sick, which is so dangerous. I could easily have choked.

I became scared that this was how I was going to feel for the rest of my life, and I knew there was no way I could live like that. I didn't realise it at the time but I had slipped into a deep depression, which wasn't helped by the fact that the police were having no luck in trying to trace my attacker.

I felt cut off from everyone and even though I knew my parents were there for me, I didn't think they could understand what I was going through. One day I had been this fun-loving girl who was dating a gorgeous man and looking forward to a career in athletics, and the next I was all alone and I felt as if all my power and happiness had been stripped away from me.

I was in pain. I had never known pain like it. I thought people who looked at me knew what had happened and I began to get paranoid, probably because I was spending a large amount of time either drunk or hungover. I felt like I smelt all the time, even though I didn't. I used to shower all the time because I was convinced that I was dirty and that people who were around me could notice it.

It seemed like everyone else was getting on with their lives, and I was trapped. I felt like no one was trying to help me. I started drinking during the day sometimes and I remember bumping into a girl I knew in town after I'd been drinking. I was clearly drunk and all she said to me was, 'Are you okay Amy? Your eyes are all over the place.' But she didn't offer to take me for a coffee or make sure I got home okay, she just walked away and left me. But then I guess how could I expect anyone to help me when they didn't know what was going on? And every time my parents had tried to help I'd pushed them away so they were probably in despair, not knowing what to do for the best.

One night several weeks after the attack I was sitting in my room drinking early one afternoon and I felt like I hit a brick wall. I gathered together all the painkillers I could find and I went to this park that's right opposite my house. I downed every single one of the painkillers with a bottle of vodka and I sat there in the cold waiting to die.

Thankfully a middle-aged couple walked past and saw me passed out so they took me to Singleton Hospital in Swansea. I had my stomach pumped and I ended up having to stay in the hospital for five days with a drip in my arm. The second day I was there I turned on my phone and I had all these messages from my mum going mad. She was asking where I was and telling me that she'd been ringing around all the hospitals trying to find me. I had given a false name and address because I didn't want my parents to see me in that state. I knew they would be worried about me, but I was ashamed.

I phoned my uncle Colin, my dad's brother, and explained everything. He's a really lovely man and a bit like a cross between Del Boy and Danny DeVito, and I knew that he wouldn't judge me for anything. At that moment he felt like the best person to call. He then phoned my parents on my behalf and explained everything to my mum. She arrived at the hospital like a shot in floods of tears and I felt terrible for being the one who had upset her. I was so embarrassed about what I'd done but all she did was hug me and tell me everything was going to be alright. I tried to explain to her why I had done what I'd done, but of course I didn't need to. She had seen how much I'd been suffering and it must have been so hard for her because I wouldn't let her help me.

Those days in hospital seemed to last forever, but the doctors had to make sure that I was totally prepared to leave and that I wasn't going to end up doing the same thing all over again. I was referred to the hospital psychologist who, despite my earlier doubts about counselling, was amazing and talked me through why I was feeling the way I was.

She explained that the fact I'd taken myself off to the park to try and commit suicide showed that I was very conscious of my action because I obviously didn't want anyone from my family to be the ones to find me. She also spoke to my mum and explained that I was very sick and that this clearly wasn't just a cry for help. My mum was in bits and when she took me home we talked and talked. I remember being hysterical and she was asking me, 'Do you want to live or do you want to die?' I was crying so much I could barely get the words out, but I managed to blurt out, 'I want to live.' And suddenly I knew that I really did.

Mum spoke to my college lecturer and explained what had been going on and he was really sympathetic. I also told the boys at college who I was friends with about why I'd been acting so weirdly and they were amazing about it. They were so caring and they promised not to tell anyone, and they didn't. It wasn't like it went around the college grapevine, they just kept it to themselves and I was so grateful. It wasn't something I wanted spread around like gossip.

After my experience with the counseller in the hospital I decided that therapy really might be able to help after all, so I started having regular counselling with a lovely woman called Ann, which helped me to deal with the attack. She was quite hippy but I really liked her approach and it didn't feel like proper counselling in a way. It felt more like I was speaking to a helpful friend who, week by week, was helping me come to terms with things. She made me do things like write a letter to my attacker. I remember one week I described him as a bird of prey who swoops down and takes their victim and then goes again, and Ann said the fact that I saw him as an animal and not a person made me really strong. I certainly didn't feel that way at the time but by seeing her each week I started to feel more like the old me and even managed to cut back on the drinking.

Chapter 5

IN TRAINING

I did managed to graduate from my HND and I spent a quiet summer getting my head together and seeing friends. Slowly but surely I started to feel better and I decided to take up the offer of a place at UWIC University, where I would be studying applied sports science and sports massage. I saw Uni as a fresh start but in all honestly that's when things went from bad to worse. Literally as soon as I left home my life fell to pieces again.

Everything started off pretty well and I moved into a house in Cardiff with two other girls who couldn't have been more different. One was an international swimmer and the other was an ex-stripper, and I think you can guess which one I got on best with. The stripper was a bit older than us and didn't want to socialize, but the swimmer and I got on really well and we went out to the student union together quite a lot.

It was the first time I had ever lived away from home and it was a real shock. It made me realise how much my parents had done for me when I lived at home. I know it's a real cliché but I didn't even know how to use the washing machine, and I lived on pasta and packet meals for months. Sometimes I totally embraced the student life and I'd have a packet of biscuits for lunch and then wine for dinner in the union. It wasn't the healthiest diet, to say the least.

My classes went really well and in between the drinking I knuckled down and worked really hard. And now when I was drinking I wasn't doing it to forget, I was doing it to enjoy myself so I never went over the top with it. I did drink most nights but with other people, never alone in my bedroom.

As part of my course I got sent to do work experience massaging the Welsh rugby team for two weeks. I know a lot of women would say that there are worse jobs you can have as a lot of them are really good looking, but at the time I wasn't in the least bit interested in meeting anyone so I saw it purely as a work thing.

A lot of the team knew me from when I was doing my athletics training or from when I was dating Gavin, so they didn't see me as some sort of girlie masseuse and they knew that I was serious about what I did. They were really respectful towards me and I was very knowledgeable about what I was doing so they took me seriously. I'm not sure how another girl my age would have fared with all those manly men!

Obviously Gavin was playing for Wales at the time but thankfully I never bumped into him. I'm guessing that he knew I was around so he avoided being there when I was, which worked for me. It would have been very strange to see him and I was doing so well and feeling so much better and I didn't want anything to hamper that.

Because the work experience with the Welsh rugby team went so well I was asked to go and do two weeks work experience at the London Wasps with their fitness coaches Craig White and their defence coach, Sean Edwards.

I went to stay with my uncle in London and when I first walked into the Wasps gym the whole place went silent. While all the guys at the Welsh rugby club saw me as the girl next door and one of the lads and they were all my mates, these guys saw me as a 21-year-old woman with blonde hair and long legs. It was a totally different world to me and quite a few of them were flirty and would make cheeky little comments here and there.

Eventually they did start to see me as more than a young blonde and I ended up getting on pretty well there. Craig and Sean were really pleased with how I'd got on and said how refreshing it was that I wasn't just there to ogle the men.

Once my two weeks was up I got given references and told that I could go back and help out any time. I was so happy because it confirmed to me that sports massage was something I was really good at and I could one day make it my career. I also made friends with a few of the guys and exchanged numbers, and I did genuinely think that I would like to go back there at some point and learn more from the other masseurs.

A few days after I got back to Wales one of the Wasps players, a guy I'll call Carl, called me and said he was coming down to Cardiff for the weekend and he asked me if he could take me out for lunch. He was a really handsome guy and I'd got on really well with him. I didn't know if he was asking me out on a date or as a mate, but either way he was good company so I agreed.

He picked me up and took me out to a local restaurant and he was the perfect gentleman. I felt really safe with him and he really looked after me. Dating wasn't something I had even let myself think about for quite a while, but as I knew Carl as a friend first I felt really comfortable around him. It soon became clear that he hadn't just asked me out as a friend and we spent most of the lunch laughing and flirting. He did keep doing this really weird thing though, where he kept getting a wad of cash out of his pocket and counting it in front of me. It was like he was trying to be flash and impress me.

We started seeing more of each other and I explained to him that I wanted to take things slowly, which he was totally cool about. He came down to visit me most weekends and occasionally during the week if he could get away, and I soon started to really like him.

After a few months of seeing Carl I decided to go on the pill. We had started sleeping together and it seemed like the best option. I'd never been on it before but how hard could it be? All I had to do was take a tablet every day and there was no way I could get pregnant. It was so simple. Only, it wasn't.

Because I was still doing my running training every morning I was pushing myself as much as possible in order to build up lactic tolerance. Quite often after running people are sick where their lactic acid has built up, and because this had been happening to me for years I didn't think anything of it. What I didn't know, having not read the instructions, was that being sick can stop the pill from working effectively. When my next period didn't arrive on time I brushed it aside, thinking it was probably to do with me working out too hard. But when it still hadn't arrived a few weeks later I panicked and went and bought a pregnancy test.

I still remember the moment when I saw the two blue lines develop on the test as clearly as if it were yesterday. I was crouched on the floor of the bathroom of my student house virtually praying for only one line to go blue. When both came up clear as day there was no denying it – I was pregnant with Carl's baby.

I didn't know whether to laugh or cry. Laugh with the ridiculousness of it all: I was 21, Carl and I had only been seeing each other for around six months, I didn't want a baby. Or cry, for the very same reasons.

I knew I had to see Carl as soon as possible and tell him the not-too-happy news, so I immediately drove to London and went to stay with my uncle. Again, he came to the rescue and phoned my parents and told them on my behalf because I couldn't face it. I had messed up. Again.

I desperately wanted to tell Carl face to face about the baby, and although we certainly weren't ready to have a child together and had never even discussed it, I did think that he would be there for me and support me in whatever I decided to do.

I called him as soon as I arrived at my uncle's and he seemed a bit off with me when I said that I was in London and wanted to see him. He told me that he was too busy to meet up and asked me why I sounded weird, and why I'd travelled all that way without bothering to check if he was around first. When I asked him when he'd be free he replied, 'Probably not for a while. Maybe a couple of weeks or so. I've got a lot on at the moment.'

I virtually begged him to see me but he kept saying that he was too busy, so in the end I blurted out, 'I'm pregnant.' I won't forget the next words out of his mouth for as long as I live. While I sat there crying on the phone, without even pausing for breath he shouted down the phone, 'Well I don't want it, get rid of it. My girlfriend will go mad.' I went into total shock. Of course I had no idea he had a girl-friend. I thought *I* was his girlfriend. He just laughed and said, 'You must have known I've got a girl-friend? I'm 32 for God's sake, you're 21. What did you think was going to happen between us?'

I burst into tears. I was inconsolable. How could I not have seen that coming? Looking back I had never once stayed at his house. Either he came to mine or on the rare occasions I came to London we would stay at one of his friend's houses or in a hotel, but I never ever questioned it. He always said that he was having work done on his place but of course his girlfriend was living there. I thought he genuinely cared about me and I loved him so much.

I told my uncle about the conversation and he said to me, 'You've got some decisions to make here. I'll support you in whatever you want to do.' He was amazing and I knew that he was one man I could actually rely on.

My mobile started ringing and when I saw it was Carl I was tempted to throw it at the wall, but I wanted to hear what he had to say. Of course I was hoping that he would say he would leave his girl-friend and be with me, but that was never going to happen. Instead he said that he hadn't meant to get angry and that he wanted to see me and talk. He came to pick me up at my uncle's house and we went for a drive. He didn't even take me for a drink or to get something to eat, we just drove around while he told me what an awful effect having a baby would have on his life. He never once asked me how I was or what I wanted. Then again, even if he had asked I don't know what I would have said. I had no idea.

I certainly felt like I was too young to have a baby, but like it or not I was pregnant and I couldn't even consider having an abortion. As far as I was concerned I would get through this somehow. Carl, however, had a very different view of it. He told me in no uncertain terms that he expected me to have an abortion as soon as possible and that I wasn't to tell anyone that I as pregnant. It was as if he was really ashamed of me.

The most ridiculous thing is that I was so in love with him I still ended up sleeping with him a couple of times after that awful day. I was secretly hoping that he would change his mind and leave his girl-friend to be with me and we would look after the baby together. I was so naïve! I was in bed with him one time and he started shouting 'die' at my stomach. Needless to say that was the moment when I knew my little fantasy wasn't going to become reality.

The one thing Carl did do was offer to pay for the abortion and also for me to have counselling afterwards. I think he would have given me any amount of money if I'd asked for it just to ensure I didn't bring our baby into the world.

I was under no illusions about how hard it would be to bring up a baby on my own, but I just couldn't bear the thought of a termination. I came up with a plan that I could have the baby and my parents could look after it while I finished Uni. I could move back home and be there in the mornings and evenings, and they could care for it during the day. I spoke to my parents and they agreed that in the circumstances it would be the best option. They assured me that we would be able to work things out between us all and I felt like I'd made the right choice.

I called Carl the next day and told him I was keeping the baby. He was driving at the time and he said to me, 'I don't want to speak to you ever again,' and put the phone down on me. His friend Steve then called me and told me again that Carl wanted nothing to do with the baby or me. Then he said, 'One of my ex-girlfriends has had an abortion and it's no big deal.' He even went on to describe to me what happens during the operation. I told him never to contact me again and I put down the phone. What a horrible, horrible thing to do. It may have been 'no big deal' to him, but this was my baby he was talking about.

I wanted some space to think about things so I headed back to my student flat in Cardiff. I was only there a day when I got a call from a number I didn't know. When I answered the phone this girl said in a really sweet voice, 'Oh hi Amy, it's Carl's girlfriend here. Carl told me what happened and that you were pregnant. What I need to know is how long you've been seeing him?' We had a brief conversation during which she told me that she'd been with him for far longer than me, that Carl had a five-year-old child that he never saw and that he was never going to leave her for me. I just kept thinking, 'Has this girl got no self-respect? Why the hell is she calling me?' I was so angry.

After that Carl seemed to totally change. It was almost like he'd had a massive change of heart. He was open about the fact that he didn't still want the baby, but he said that he did want to be with me whatever. His girlfriend moved out of his flat and he was single again and I was the person he'd chosen to be with, so like a fool I took him back. I can't believe I was so stupid but I was still so needy and I wanted him to love me like I loved him.

Every time I saw him he talked about the baby and how it would just get in the way of us being together. He would say that maybe it would be good to wait so we could have children together in the future when we were both ready for it. It was almost like he was brainwashing me and he would literally go on for hours about how my life would never be the same and it would be the end of my fun. I pointed out that I would still be able to have a life and a career like so many other women but he just laughed at me and said, 'You're 21, and you're going to be tied to a cot for a good few years.'

In the end he wore me down so much I agreed to have an abortion. Maybe he was right? Maybe it was just bad timing and we would be better off waiting until I was settled in a career and he was in the right place to have a child. Although I allowed Carl to arrange everything I refused to take a penny from him and I payed for the operation myself.

He booked me in to a place called Marie Stopes clinic in Ealing and I travelled up to London the night before and stayed at his house for the first time. I thought the fact that he was happy to have me in his house was a definite sign that he wanted to make a go of things after the operation. Some of his girlfriend's stuff was still around but he explained that she hadn't had time to pick it all up yet. I even remember laughing at a really horrible pair of shoes that were in the wardrobe and he laughed and said, 'Yes, she doesn't have the best style!'

I didn't tell anyone – not my parents, my friends or even my uncle – that I was going for the abortion because I didn't want anyone else's opinions. I knew someone could very easily have talked me out of it and I needed to stick with the decision that I had made.

I woke up on the morning of the operation feeling sick, unable to believe what I was about to do. Carl drove me to the clinic, and then he sat in the waiting room of the clinic, giggling as he read a magazine without a care in the world. He even arrogantly suggested that he should give a false name for him in case someone there recognised him. Despite everything he was still thinking about himself, when all I wanted him to do was hold my hand.

I had to go for a scan and had a urine test and the doctor told me that I was nine weeks and 2 days pregnant. That was much further along that I expected so it came as a bit of a shock. I was ready to back out there and then but I was too scared. I thought of Carl sitting down in the waiting room and how mad he would go.

The actual operation was taking place in another building so we walked over to it and sat in yet another sparse waiting room. There was nothing at all private about the whole experience. Everyone knew what everyone else was there for, and it felt like everyone was waiting to go to the electric chair. There were rows of chairs with these terrified girls sitting on them, and when their names were called they would walk in and then come out a short while later in a wheelchair.

When my name was called I had tears in my eyes as I walked towards the nurse. This wasn't what I wanted. Everyone else's partners had kissed them goodbye and said they'd be there for them when they got out, but there was none of that with Carl. He just sat there reading and he barely even looked up. As I walked up the stairs I turned around and looked at him and something inside of me said: 'I'm never going to see this man again.'

I walked into the operating theatre and the doctor introduced himself and then went to shake my hand, but I couldn't do it. I couldn't shake his hand, I felt too ashamed. He explained to me that I would be put under conscious sedation, which is where you can't feel anything but you're wide-awake and aware of what's going on. The doctor moved towards me and put an injection in my arm, which terminates the pregnancy. I look down in horror and started saying 'no, no, no', but it was too late. Still to this day I can hear the noises as they operated on me. It makes me feel sick to my stomach when I think about it.

Once it was over I went and lay on a bed and I texted Carl. He'd said he had some things to do so he was going to leave and then come back and get me when I was ready, so I asked him to come and collect me. He told me he'd come back in an hour and half. I wondered what could possibly be so important that he had to do it then and could leave me all alone after something like that? I soon found out.

It turned out that he'd gone back to his house and put all my things in a bag. He handed it to me and said that he would take me anywhere I wanted to go but we couldn't go back to his house and he never wanted me to go there again.

I broke down sobbing and told him to take me to my uncle's house. When he dropped me off he didn't even bother to walk me to the door. I remember my uncle telling me that when he looked at Carl as he sat in his car he knew that something had happened, because he had a look of relief on his face. I didn't understand it. I had done what he wanted, I had tried to keep him happy and still he didn't want me. I stayed at my uncle's for a few days to recover before I headed back to Cardiff. I did try calling Carl but he never took my calls. I left him messages saying I desperately needed to speak to him, but he didn't call me back. He was the first man I had trusted since the attack and he'd hurt me all over again.

I later found out through a friend of Carl's that I was the third girl he'd taken for an abortion. I also found out that he and and his girlfriend had never actually split up. All that time he had carried on sleeping with me and he was still with her the entire time. For all I know they plotted the whole 'Carl and I getting back together' scenario in a bid to get me to have an abortion.

Carl is probably seen as an upstanding member of the community, but he's a horrible man. I pity any woman who crosses his path. And I also pity – in the words of Carl's best mate – 'the long suffering girlfriend'.

Chapter 6

WALKING AWAY

I decided that the best thing for me to do was to go back to University, throw myself into work and try and take my mind off things. I was completely heartbroken about the operation, and also about losing Carl all over again. Even though he was an awful person, I felt lonely not having him around. Not that he was ever really there for me, I guess.

I sank into a deep depression again and I would spend ages on the Internet every day researching abortions. I became obsessed about all the minor details. I just couldn't get past what I'd done. I decided that everything about my life needed to change. The first thing I did – just because it was quick and easy to do – was go and see my hairdresser friend Dominic and get him to cut all of my hair off and bleach it blonde. It was almost like I wanted to be someone else. I had spent so much of my life being seen as one of the boys and I was always considered to be so tough and capable of looking after myself, but really I was just a vulnerable young girl who wanted looking after. Carl had even said to me after the abortion, 'Oh, you're a big strong girl. I've had a girl pregnant in the past and she was a lot smaller than you and she recovered really quickly.' Everyone thought I could handle anything. I guess that even though I cried a lot, I hadn't really allowed anyone to see that side of me before. I was so busy putting on a front and making out like I was strong that somewhere along the way I'd forgotten to be myself. And now it was time to do that all over again. I decided that I wanted to reinvent myself and make all the bad times go away. I wanted to be someone totally new.

My head became totally focused on the abortion and I could barely think about anything else. My Uni work started to suffer and I began missing a lot of lectures. I didn't have the same passion for the course work as I had once done. In fact, I didn't really have much of a passion for anything except alcohol. The booze had made a very unwelcome return and I had gone back to drinking alone in my room. I couldn't bear the thought of going out with other people. Thankfully I soon saw myself falling into all the same patterns as before. I knew I had to do something to get me out of the rut I was in otherwise I was just going to sink further and further into depression again.

I went along and saw my doctor and explained the situation and he prescribed me some anti-depressants. I started taking them immediately but when they didn't have the desired effect I panicked. I just wanted to feel good again and I felt like the tablets weren't doing what they should. I looked up anti-depressants on the Internet and I found a website that sold Xanax, a really strong antidepressant which treats panic and anxiety. I used my student loan to buy a few packets and all of a sudden I was on a roll. It was so easy to buy prescription medication and once I got one lot, I wanted more.

I found another website that sold beta-blockers and I ordered a few packets of those as well. It's illegal to buy them over the Internet in this country but I ordered them from America and again, it was so simple, no questions asked. Beta-blockers help you stay calm and focused but you can still work when you're on them so they sounded perfect for me. Then, just for good measure, I bought some Valium to help me sleep. My sleep patterns had been really erratic which I knew wasn't helping with my moods, so I decided they would be a good solution. Valium literally knocks you out and they would provide me with another escape from the world.

I was like a kid in a sweet shop when all the drugs arrived and I opened them all and spread them across my bed. At last I was going to feel better. I would be like my old self again. All the hurt and pain would go away and I would be fun Amy: the tomboy who loves sports and was always laughing at ridiculous things. I had always been young at heart – I guess that's a nice way of saying naïve – and I desperately wanted my innocence and fun-loving side back.

I started taking the tablets, along with the ones my doctor had prescribed me, and I started to feel zoned out a lot of the time. I was either on this fake high on the anti-depressants or leveling myself out with beta-blockers and Valium.

My spending span way out of control and my student loan was very close to running out. In my quest to be more girlie I was also having my hair done all the time, buying expensive make up and splashing out on clothes. I thought nothing of going to Karen Millen and spending £125 on a top. I'd never done those things before and I was loving it.

My lecture attendance was also getting increasingly bad. I would go and sit and listen to what the tutors were saying, but it was a case of 'the lights are there but there's no one home'. I didn't take anything in and my mind was always elsewhere. Incredibly, in my really dark times, my thoughts always turned to Carl. I would stare at my phone for ages willing him to call. I honestly believed that one day he would call and tell me that he'd made a mistake, that the abortion didn't matter and that he wanted to be with me. I waited for that phone call for months, but it never came.

I got into a routine of having vodka and Valium to sleep most nights, and then a Xanax when I woke up in the morning to perk me up. And just in case I wasn't taking enough medication, I decided to start on Phedra-Cut as well. It's like a herbal form of speed that you can buy in health shops and it's used to keep your weight down because it speeds up your metabolism. The anti-depressants the doctor had given me had made me put on weight, and I was no longer training constantly so I wasn't burning it off like I always had done in the past.

I was so desperate to be seen as feminine at that point. I wanted my hair to look pretty and I wanted the weight and the muscles to go. I wanted someone to come along and sweep me off my feet and make me feel loved and protected again and I thought they would only do that if I looked perfect. As I said before, I had never really given my body much thought, but when I put on weight I didn't like it one bit and it made me feel even less confident.

I walked around in a daze half the time not really aware of what was going on around me. I would spend hours – sometimes even days – sat in my room on my own and I would only leave to go to the toilet or get more alcohol. I didn't really bother with food. I stopped going to the student union, and I didn't party at all or even really socialise with anyone else. My flatmates must have thought I was insane but not once did they ask if I was okay or offer to help me. But as always, I didn't ask for any help and I was very offhand with them, so I guess it's very hard to help someone if it seems like they don't want it.

It soon became evident to me and everyone around me that it was going to be impossible for me to stay at Uni. It was pointless. I had fallen so far behind with my studies there was no way I could catch up. And quite frankly, I didn't want to. All my ambitions had melted away and I wanted to take what I thought was the easy option – booze and prescription drugs. If only I'd known just how wrong I was.

Things came to a head around the end of February and I knew I couldn't handle Uni any longer, so I literally packed my stuff up and got into my car and drove away. Once I made the decision I was gone within hours and I didn't even say goodbye to my flatmates. I just upped and left and moved back home to my parents' house. I thought that I would at least have home comforts there, and maybe be able to get more control over my life.

Of course my parents were disappointed that I had made the decision to leave Uni, but they didn't give me a hard time about it. I think it was obvious from how I looked that I was finding things difficult. I realise it must have been hard for them seeing me like that as well but they just thought I looked pale and tired because of lack of sleep. They had no idea that I was taking so many pills and drinking so much.

After a couple of weeks at home I started to get itchy feet and wonder what the hell I was going to do with my future. It's surprising I could even think about the future, to be fair. I wanted to go out and feel alive again, and I wanted to see a friend – anyone! It had been so long since I'd been out on the town and felt like a normal twenty something, so I called an old friend of mine, Danny, and he invited me to stay with him in Birmingham there and then. It was quite late and it would have taken me a while to get there but he was insistent and laughed, 'Come on Amy girl, things done on the spur of the moment are always the most fun!' How could I resist?

I jumped in my car and headed for Birmingham. As soon as I got there we dumped my bags at Danny's and headed straight into town to hit the bars. For the first time in months I felt like there was light at the end of the tunnel. I was having a good time. A proper, full-on, fun evening. Danny made me feel like I still had a real mate and it was so good to escape from everything for a night. I told Danny all about what had happened with Carl and I remember him saying to me, 'You need to text him and tell him that you don't need him. You need to say that you've moved on, and that Danny is showing you what the world is really like, and it's going to be fun.' I was laughing my head off. Danny had a girl-friend so there was nothing between us at all, but I felt like I had a genuine friend and he gave me some hope that night that I could pick myself up and start again. I'll always be grateful to him for that.

I don't know what I was expecting to happen after that, it wasn't as if my life was magically going to turn around, but at least it showed me that I could enjoy myself. I went back to my parents the following day feeling more positive than I had in a long time. All of a sudden there was a world out there waiting for me. There were parties to go to and laughs to be had.

After a few weeks of lazing around the house my mum started asking me what I was going to do with my life. I had a long think about the future and I decided to go back to training. I spoke to a guy called Terry, who I had known for some years as he was the director of performance and coaching in Wales, and explained my plan. He knew everything that had been going on with me and he was aware of everything I'd been through, and based on that he said that he thought it was a bit early for me to go back to proper training. Instead he said I was welcome to go down to the training ground and hang out with everyone and ease myself back into it.

I seemed like a good option and he was right; I

wasn't mentally or physically equipped to throw myself back into everything so a slow burn sounded like the best option. I did feel a bit apprehensive about going back after so long but as Terry introduced me to Linford Christie – who was at the club coaching Jamie Baulch, Darren Campbell and Paul Gray at the time – I felt totally at ease. Linford was so nice to me and he really inspired me, so I got a huge kick out of watching him training some of the UK's best athletes.

I started going back to the gym quite regularly and I was building up my training bit by bit. Linford was always shouting at me when he saw me running saying, 'Come on, I want to see you really working!' He wasn't my coach but he knew I had problems so he was really supportive and always tried to involve me in things. In fact, all the guys did. They were all friends of Danny's and he'd told them to watch out for me so they were lovely to me. I felt like I really fitted in there and I looked forward to my sessions.

It felt really cool that I was hanging out with Linford because he has always been my idol. In fact, my uncle had approached him at Gatwick airport several years before and got his autograph for me because I liked him so much. I've still got it at home. It's a paper plate that says 'To Amy Lou, with lots of love Linford.' It was just after he had won the Barcelona Olympics so I was over the moon. Then here I was with him telling me jokes, and I always used to laugh and say, 'What's in your lunchbox today?' It seemed so crazy.

Sadly I realised after being around the training club for a while that I had lost all interest in competing and I came to the conclusion that my dreams of being an international athlete had crumbled. My heart just wasn't in it any more. I still carried on turning up to the club for the company, and I also liked the buzz of exercising, but I no longer felt like I was aiming towards a goal like I had done in the past. It was more for fun and the company of other people than anything else.

I had no money and no job, but I still had somewhere to go, and that was really important to me at the time. Once again I had become one of the lads and it was so nice to have people that I knew would be there for me. But soon what was now a dependence on prescription drugs got in the way. I was taking so many pills that it became almost impossible to train because I was so up and down, and I decided to turn my back on running for good. I had to draw a line underneath it because in a way I was trying to get back my old life, and I knew deep down that wasn't going to happen. It all started to feel a bit fake after a while and I didn't see any point in trying to recapture what I'd lost. I think a lot of that was paranoia kicking in as I used to worry all the time that people would think I was sad for trying to be a good athlete again, when it was clear I had no chance of ever being how I used to be again.

After I stopped the training for good I had nothing else to do but spend time around my house. I had hit a real low and didn't have any enthusiasm for anything, and despite my parents encouraging me to go out and find work, I just didn't have the inclination to do it.

Although I was taking enough anti-depressants to make an elephant smile, I still felt total despair, probably due to the amount I was drinking and the fact that any sleep I did get wasn't a natural sleep, but drug or booze induced. I would take Xanax and Phedra-Cut as soon as I got up to give me energy and try and lift my mood, but whatever I did, I couldn't stop thinking about Carl and the abortion. It got to the point where I was almost obsessive and was convinced that him coming back to me was the only thing that would save me.

The next couple of months were completely unproductive. I was either lying on the sofa watching TV, hiding in my room listening to music or arguing with my parents because I wasn't making any effort to get a job. I didn't even want to go into town in case I bumped into anyone and they thought what a loser I was for dropping out of Uni. I was a mess of a girl and I kept getting panicky about stupid things. I felt like I was trapped inside my own head and nothing I could do would stop that. I didn't understand why the tablets I was taking weren't making me feel normal, but looking back I was mixing them with a lot of booze, and I'm also pretty sure that the combination I was taking wasn't the best.

One day I woke up and decided that I couldn't carry on the way I had been. Life was just too hard. I was in a total state and I had nothing to live for. I knew what I had to do. I waited until it got dark, and then in an echo of my earlier suicide attempt I drank loads of vodka, took loads of pills and went and sat in the very same park as I had done before while I waited for them to kick in. I wanted to die. I thought that this time I had a better chance of it actually working. As it was dark it was far less likely that anyone would find me.

It's weird that I went back to exactly the same place to try and commit suicide again after being saved there last time, because I knew for sure that I really didn't want to be saved again. But like history repeating itself, once again someone found me lying on the grass and took me to hospital. I had my stomach pumped and I ended up having to stay in hospital for a couple of days. But I remember feeling disappointed that someone had found me. I didn't feel like I deserved to be rescued. I didn't feel like I deserved to live.

My parents were horrified and so upset when they

came to see me in the hospital. They couldn't believe that it had happened again. My mum said she wished she'd seen the signs, but what signs? How can you tell when someone is about to take their own life? You can hardly follow someone around all day making sure they're not squirreling away tablets or swiping knives from the kitchen drawer. She had tried to reach out to me so many times but I was very good at convincing her that I was okay and would even talk about my hopes for the future. I hated the fact that I had upset my family because I knew how much they loved me. I know that people say that suicide is a selfish act but I honestly thought that by killing myself I would be doing them a favour. I thought I was doing everyone a favour.

Right before I took the overdose I had texted Carl's friend Andy and wrote: 'Tell Carl I really love him and he's the only one for me. I'm sorry.' Andy then showed it to Carl and he immediately knew that something was wrong. He asked some mutual friends how I was and found out what had happened, and two weeks after I got out of hospital he called me. He wasn't particularly sympathetic or nice. I felt like he was just calling me to clear his conscience and he didn't offer to come and see me or anything. If felt weird speaking to him again as I had built him up into an almost God-like figure, but he sounded almost pathetic on the phone. Like he was going through the motions and saying what he felt he should say to make me feel better. Nothing he said was from the heart, and I wonder if he was just making sure I wouldn't try anything like that again so that he could relax and get on with his life without having to worry or feel guilty. In a way speaking to him actually helped because it made me see him for the self-obsessed wimp that he is.

I had some counselling after my suicide attempt but it didn't help in the same way it did the first time around. It just made me cry a lot and I got to the point where I wondered if I could actually cry any more. I think sometimes with things you have to say 'okay, this has happened, I'll put it in a box and file it away', but instead I wanted to get to the bottom of why Carl was so awful to me. But there was no answer. He was a horrible person and he didn't care about hurting people. I didn't need a counsellor to tell me that.

Chapter 7

BRIGHT LIGHTS, BIG CITY

After the second suicide attempt I felt like I needed a fresh start in a new city and my uncle very kindly said that I could move in with him in Wandsworth for as long as I wanted while I sorted myself out a job and a permanent place to stay. I had nothing to stay in Wales for.

My athletics career was over, my Uni course was no more and I felt so emotionally battered from everything. I wasn't naïve enough to think that the streets of London were paved with gold, but I wanted to escape and be somewhere where nobody knew me and I could reinvent myself in a way. No one would know about the things that had happened to me and I wouldn't have to explain myself to anyone. I could be as anonymous as I wanted and the idea excited me no end.

My parents weren't very happy about me leaving home as they thought I was still too fragile to make such a big step, but of course I thought I knew what was best for me. And after I spoke to them about it and explained everything they agreed that it would do me good and that I needed to get away from all the bad memories. I didn't know what I was going to do work wise or anything and I didn't really mind. I hadn't really had many jobs up until that point and I wasn't really qualified for anything, but I decided to take my chances.

It didn't bother me one bit that Carl was in London, and I certainly didn't worry about bumping into him. London is such a big place. The chances of seeing someone by chance are very slim, especially as he lived over the other side of town from my uncle. Obviously I knew all the places he used to hang out so if I had wanted to see him I could have done, but that wasn't even an option. I was no longer going to let him figure in my life in any way.

I had been to London quite a few times in the past so I wasn't intimidated about moving up even though it's about ten times as busy and frantic as Wales. I didn't have any friends there to speak of, but I knew it wouldn't take me long to get to know people in such a huge place. And at least I knew that my uncle and auntie would be there for me if I needed them.

It felt strange packing up all my stuff from home and loading it into my car. I had moved out of home before when I went to Uni, but this felt quite final and I crammed as much as I could into my boot and back seat. It was almost as if I knew that this time it was for good and I would probably never live back at home with my parents again. This was going to be the next big step for me and I was as nervous as I was excited. I was 21 and it was time for me to spread my wings and get out there and start living. Nearly dying again meant that I'd had to make a decision about whether I wanted to give up completely or move on and make something of myself, and somehow I found the strength in myself to start caring about myself again.

My uncle gave me my own room in his house and I soon set about making it homely. In those first few weeks my uncle and auntie couldn't do enough for me and I didn't miss Wales one bit. I loved being able to walk down the road with no one knowing who I was. Back home everyone knew everyone else's business so it was such a nice change. Sometimes I'd leave the house and walk for miles safe in the knowledge that to everyone else I was just this tall, skinny blonde girl and no one knew my story. And my new story was about to begin.

I cut my ties with everyone when I moved to London. As soon as I got over the Severn Bridge as I was driving up the M4 I decided to delete everyone's phone numbers in my mobile, apart from my family's. I decided that my past was going to stay in my past, and that meant all the people who had played a part – no matter how big or small – in the old Amy. Soon my phone would be filled with new numbers of new friends and I didn't need reminding of where I'd come from.

I started looking around for work and I landed a job in a small boutique hotel called Vancouver Studios in Bayswater, working on the reception. All I did all day was check people in and out and hand over keys. It was really busy in the morning and sometimes late afternoon, but then I would have to sit there all day with nothing to do, bored out of my mind. There's nothing worse than having too much time on your hands as it means you've got lots of time to think, which has never been a good thing for me. My mind just goes into overdrive.

Because the hotel was so small there were only about four other people working there and none of them were very sociable so it wasn't like it was easy to make friends. My plan to get out and enjoy London nightlife hadn't quite worked out and after about a month of being in London I started to feel quite lonely.

I would walk home from work in the evening and see everyone else going out to have fun, and all I did was go and sit and watch TV with my auntie and uncle wishing I had someone to go to the pub with. I used to sit there thinking: 'I'm living in London and I'm bored. This is ridiculous!' I came to London for an adventure, so I decided to go in search of one.

I had always known that I couldn't live at my uncle's house forever, and once I'd managed to save up a bit of money I decided to try and find a flat of my own. I found a place in Putney through a website and accepted it straight away. It wasn't very big but it had everything I needed, and within a week I was living in my first ever place on my own.

The first night there was so strange. I had the radio on full blast and I was dancing around singing at the top of my voice just because I could. There was no one there to tell me what I could and couldn't do and I felt this incredible sense of freedom that I'd never had before. I bought myself a bottle of wine and some snacks and that was like my very own house warming party.

After paying for a month's rent and the deposit on the flat I didn't have a lot of money and what I did have went on clothes, food and drink, and I decided that a TV was a luxury I couldn't afford so in those first few weeks I was constantly listening to the radio. I wasn't going out at all because I was yet to make any friends, so I used to pass the time in the quiet evenings by drinking. Most nights I used to sit in listening to music and drinking a bottle of wine. Then it became two bottles of wine.

Thinking about it, if I'd saved up the money I spent on booze I probably could have afforded a TV. Especially when a month or so later the two bottles of wine a night became a bottle of vodka.

The crazy teenager in me had been unleashed at last and I could do whatever I wanted, drink whatever I wanted and eat whatever I wanted and there was no one there to tell me off. I lived on cheap packet meals, and when you opened my fridge all you saw were bottles of booze. Other people have bottles of Evian in their fridge, I had wine and vodka.

The drinking got to be a real habit and there were times when I could wake up in the morning and have a glass of wine without even thinking about it. No one told me I couldn't! I was hoping that the drinking would give me the confidence to go out and meet people because I still felt very lonely.

I decided that now I was having a new start it was as good a time as any to come off the anti-depressants. I was taking way too many and I'd always promised myself that they were a short-term fix. And anyway, the booze alone was making me sleep now, I didn't need the Valium as well. But of course I didn't do it the sensible way of cutting down slowly, I just decided to stop altogether so the next week was pretty rough. I kept feeling sick and dizzy and a bit spaced, I guess from where my body was readjusting. I experienced crashing highs and lows and every day started to become a bit of a struggle but I knew it would pass once all the drugs were out of my system.

I was coming to the end of my tether with the

hotel job. I was so bored all the time and no one really spoke to me. It wasn't exactly leading the dynamic London life I had envisaged. One day just before I was due to leave for my shift I decided that enough was enough, so I went to a local internet café and sent them an email saying that I wasn't coming in that day and, in fact, I wouldn't be going in ever again. I just couldn't face it. I felt like I'd done well lasting as long as I had done so I didn't feel in the least bit guilty. It was one of those places where people only ever stayed for a few months so I'm sure they were used to it.

I decided that the best thing to do would be to look for work around Putney. That way I would have no travel costs and it would give me a chance to get to know people locally. The very next day I got up and walked around the town, and found myself two jobs in local pubs. I literally just walked in, told the managers I was looking for a job and landed some shifts. I was excited because it meant that I finally got to interact with people. I could listen to other people's problems and they could listen to mine, and I'd make loads of friends in no time.

The great thing was that the pubs were right opposite each other and the managers knew each other so there was never any problem with me working for both, and I would flit between the two. The customers were a mixture of young and old, and mainly men, some of whom spent all day sitting at the bar chatting to me. They were so welcoming and I soon got to know the regulars. I became like a part of the family and someone would always walk me home after my shift if it was dark. I soon started to feel a lot happier and more settled.

There was this one guy who was a bit odd who used to come into both the pubs and sit there and stare at me. Half the time he didn't even buy a drink, he'd just pretend to use the toilet and then stand around looking at me and smiling. He had randomly asked me out when I was walking down a street near my flat a couple of weeks before and now he kept turning up all the time. It was really creepy, especially as I was still quite nervous around men, and something about him wasn't right.

If I saw him in town he would follow me and try to talk to me, and I used to be as polite as possible but he made me feel quite uncomfortable. Then one day I walked out of my flat and he was sitting on the stairs waiting for me. It all got a bit much so one of the guys from the pub contacted the police and I never saw him again thankfully. But I did wonder if I was becoming some kind of magnet for strange men. I often had men coming up to me and asking me out or trying to talk to me, but I thought it must just be what happened in London. It had certainly never happened to me in Wales.

There were a couple of young guys who used to

come into the pub who I became really friendly with called Stefan and Lloyd, and we used to go over to each other's houses and hang out quite a lot. It felt nice to have friends again after so long and it made me realise just how lonely I'd been.

Even when things got tough and throughout all the loneliness I never felt like I wanted to go back to Wales. I didn't even give my old life a second thought and although I spoke to my parents pretty regularly, I didn't even ask about life back home. To me it was a million miles away.

Of course the problem with working in pubs was that it was even easier for me get hold of alcohol. All the regulars would buy me drinks and there was nothing to stop me sneaking the odd free one from behind the bar here and there either. I remember we had this one function and everyone was buying me vodka all night and I was throwing them back. My boss turned round to me and said, 'Amy, have you been drinking?' because I could barely stand up. Thankfully he thought it was funny, but I could easily have lost my job over it. It didn't put me off drinking on the job though. I saw it as one of perks.

I'd generally have a few drinks throughout the day or night every time and then have a couple more before I went home. Sometimes I did a double shift so I'd work from eleven in the morning until eleven at night and I'd drink the whole way through. Then

I would go home and drink more. I think alcohol had always been a bit of an issue for me. I remember back in 1998 we had a school ball, and it was the first time I had ever drunk alcohol. Some friends had some wine and beer and they offered to share it with me and I ended up getting so drunk my English teacher had to drive me home. When we got to my house my mum opened the door and the teacher pushed me towards her and said, 'Mrs Bohan, your daughter.' I got into loads of trouble with my parents. I guess that set the tone for my future drinking years. I could never just stop at one.

It's weird because when I used to go out into Swansea on nights out I would often drive and it didn't bother me that I wasn't drinking, but every time I did drink I could rarely stop at a few. I guess I was an all or nothing kind of girl. But as I got older, it definitely became less of the 'nothing' and more of the 'all'.

Even if I was just drinking alone in my flat I would get completely wrecked. I would literally drink until I passed out. Sometimes I'd wake up on the sofa at five in the morning wondering why the hell I wasn't in bed, and there were even times when I passed out while sitting at the kitchen table. My hangovers weren't even that bad weirdly, and if I did have a band hangover I would just have another drink. It wasn't unusual for me have a drink when I woke up and then another one at lunchtime; usually a wine or a vodka and slimline tonic. Having a drink first thing became as normal to me as having breakfast. In fact, it was probably even more normal as I often didn't bother with breakfast.

I was worried that all the alcohol would make me put on weight and I was more conscious about how I looked than ever now I was living in London. Everyone seemed so glamorous and I wanted to feel like I fitted in. I was still taking the Phedra-Cut, which was definitely helping with my keeping the weight off, and I also started taking Xenical, which is another slimming tablet that flushes all the fat out of your body. I don't think either of them necessarily helped me lose weight, but they did stop me putting it on. I knew that without the running I used to do my body could easily have started storing fat and I was almost terrified of putting weight on. The main problem was that as Phedra-cut contains herbal speed it would often keep me awake, so I had to drink increasing amounts just to get to sleep. I was spending hundreds of pounds a month on slimming pills and booze. God knows how I managed to ever pay my rent.

I had never suffered from any kind of eating disorder before and even when I was an insecure teenager I had never really given my weight a second thought, apart from when bullies were calling me skinny. But as I got older I started to worry more and more about getting or looking fat. After the abortion I went through a phase of only eating chicken and vegetables, and only once a day at dinner time. I refused to eat anything else at all. I wonder if it was a kind of control thing. Maybe because my life felt so completely out of control that was the only thing I could have any real say in?

While I was working in the pub all those insecurities returned, hence the new slimming tablets came in. I developed a kind of phobia about food because I wanted to be perfect. While in some ways I didn't want to be attractive to men because of the things that had happened to me, I also didn't want to feel unattractive when I looked in the mirror as I was already suffering from crippling self-esteem. I know it doesn't make much sense but it was like I had a split personality and each of them wanted totally different things. I wanted to feel good about myself and I would put on nice clothes and false eyelashes and bright lipstick when I went out, but at the same time I didn't want men looking at me as anything other than a friend because I was convinced that they would hurt me in some way.

Chapter 8

WEST
END GIRL

The longer I stayed working at the pubs, the more friends I made and the more I felt like I had found my place in London. There was one guy in particular called Simon who I used to hang out with a lot. One night he suggested that we went up to town to a club called Chinawhite, which is well known as a celebrity haunt and was *the* place to go at the time. I jumped at the chance; after all, glamour and fun was what I had moved to London for.

I got dressed up in my best clothes and spent ages doing my make-up, and then I met Simon at the tube station. I was so excited because although I'd been in London for a few months by then, I hadn't been into the West End on a night out and everyone knows that's where the coolest people hang out. Simon suggested that we went for a drink first but I'd already been drinking at home and I wanted to head straight to Chinawhite. We got in there at half nine, which I now know is a ridiculously early time to get to a big London club. But on the plus side, because we were so early we got in for free. I soon found out why. We were literally the only people rattling around this huge club and I remember thinking 'what's all the fuss about? This place is dead'. When it got to be around half eleven all of a sudden the place starting filling up. Within an hour it was absolutely packed, and I was steaming drunk. It was £10 a drink, but we decided that as it wasn't something we did very often we'd go for it. And I felt like we had to spend money to fit in with everyone else. There was a really strange mix of people in there, from ridiculously rich, flashy businessmen to girls in tiny white dresses and skyscraper heels who looked quite cheap but were clearly out to try and meet a rich man. There were a few celebrities in there as well, but I had never really been into the celebrity world so although I recognised them, I didn't have a clue who they were. There was one guy who the girls were flocking round and I asked Simon who he was. He said he was a celeb agent who managed a lot of high profile stars and he had become famous off the back of it. These girls were literally throwing themselves at him and I couldn't understand it as he wasn't in the least bit attractive. I didn't realise it at the time but of course they were only cosying up to him because they wanted to try and become famous. It certainly wasn't his looks or his charm that was winning them over.

Simon and I danced all night and had an amazing time. I was having such a brilliant time that I never wanted to leave. At one point I went to the toilet and this woman started talking to me. She was draped in diamonds and smelt really strongly of a musky perfume, and she was clearly quite drunk because her eyes had that pissed, tired look about them. As soon as I walked in she cornered me and started asking me what I did for a living. I explained that I'd just moved to London and that I was working in a couple of bars and she said to me, 'Forget that, I can make you some real money. Give me a call.' She pressed her business card into my hand and when I looked down all I saw was the word 'escort'. She obviously could see that I looked concerned so she told in this soothing voice that all it involved was going out for nice dinners and chatting to men, but I wasn't that stupid. No one makes a lot of money from sitting around politely chatting to guys; there's always something else involved.

As soon as I left the toilet I ran up to Simon and said, 'We're going!' For some reason the woman really freaked me out. I don't know what I expected a big London club to be but it wasn't like that. Sure, this was a place where celebrities came to be papped and millionaires came to pull young girls, but I didn't expect it to be the kind of place where women offered you work as a glorified prostitute.

I should have known there and then that going clubbing could lead me into danger and that there were some seedy people on the scene, but I put it down to being a one-off. And anyway, apart from that woman, Simon and I had an amazing night and we were already planning our next big night out.

Over the next few weeks Simon and I went to Funky Buddha and Movida and we started hanging out on the party scene pretty regularly. It was always the same routine; we'd get there early so we could get in for free, then get drunk and dance all night. We always got talking to random people and we soon started to recognise the same faces. Everyone was always drunk so it wasn't hard to get a conversation going with people, and one night while I was in Movida I got talking to this guy called Chris, who was a photographer. He asked if I was a model and when I said no he suggested that I go to a model agency and see if I could land a contract. He offered to take me to a fashion agency to see if they would take me on and I was completely taken aback and very flattered. Chris seemed like a genuinely nice guy and although I'd never thought of modelling before, I knew it would be a good and easy way of making some money. As long as it wasn't the dodgy kind of modelling!

I arranged to meet Chris a couple of days later

and I half expected him not to turn up. He took me along to the agency and they looked me up and down a lot, shrugged and told me that they had lots of girls on their books who looked like me. I felt a bit disheartened but then they said they'd take me on and send me out on castings to see if I could get any work. It wasn't really the enthusiastic response I was hoping for. I wasn't expecting to be hailed as the new Kate Moss or anything but it would have been nice if they'd at least seemed like they thought I was attractive. Chris assured me that it was normal for agencies to be like that, so I signed up, went home and waited for them to call me about any appointments they wanted to send me on.

I didn't have to wait long for the call and within a day they'd left a message on my mobile giving me instructions about where I had to be and when. I was still working in the pubs and I knew I would have to fit the castings in around that, but I was determined to make it work. Modelling can be a very lucrative business and I had visions of myself with a wardrobe of designer clothes and VIP tables at some of the best clubs in town. But as I was to discover, the reality couldn't have been more different.

Every model who is starting out, and even some of the biggest models in the world, have to go on castings. It basically means that you have to travel to wherever the designer is based so that the organisers of the photo shoots or catwalk shows can see if you'd be right for their campaign. They evaluate whether or not you're what they're looking for and then report back to your agency. If you're lucky, they'll book you. If not, it can be one of many, many wasted journeys.

I didn't get any work from the first few castings I went to, but I still got sent out on more and sometimes I would be out from eight in the morning until eight at night running around London hoping that someone would want to pay me to model their clothes. There was absolutely nothing glamorous about it whatsoever. Some of the places I had to travel to were on the outskirts of London in grotty warehouses, and I even went to castings in people's houses.

It was always the same routine. You had to queue up with a load of other aspiring models, then stand in front of up to ten people while they looked you over and asked you questions about your hip or bra size. All the models were treated like cattle. It was like a conveyor belt, and when it was your turn to step on it you had to prepare yourself for the worst. Sometimes you had to try on clothes and walk up and down in front of them, and other times you had to stand there in your underwear while they scrutinised you. Sometimes they'd pinch bits of your flesh to see if you had any fat on you. And they didn't hold back in telling you what they thought.

I got told that my hair was a mess, my teeth were too big, my boobs were too small . . . you name it, I heard it.

For someone whose self-esteem was pretty much rock bottom anyway, it really wasn't the best business for me to be in. I remember one designer telling me when I was about eight stone I was too fat and I shot back, 'Well if you want a 14 year-old with a drug problem you go and get one.' Not surprisingly, I didn't get that job.

I was going on tons of castings but the problem was that I wasn't actually getting booked for many jobs. It was like I had a full time job schlepping around London being insulted, only I wasn't being paid for it. I had to miss loads of shifts at the pub in order to go to all the appointments and even though both my bosses were understanding, I was losing out on a lot of money and I was worried about how I would pay the rent.

After a few weeks I was finally booked for my first job and I was so happy. It was for a hair salon and the job involved me getting my hair done and then walking up and down a catwalk to show it off. I was worried that everyone would be snobby but the people were so nice and I had a really fun day, so I started to think much more positively about modelling. I was really skint at that point so I was waiting for the payment to come in. But when the cheque arrived, after the agency fees had been taken off, it was £60. Hardly worth it considering all the work I'd put in.

I had no money left in the bank and what little money I had in cash was going on my rent, the slimming pills and alcohol. I was barely even buying food or clothes at that point and it was hard living from day to day. I realise that alcohol and slimming pills aren't exactly a necessity to everyone, but they were for me for the sake of my sanity.

I got booked for another fashion show a little while later at Kensington Olympia. I remember thinking that everyone looked really beautiful and I felt like I shouldn't have really been there. The castings had knocked my confidence more than ever so I felt like a real ugly duckling. It was very different from the hair show that I had done. It was a much bigger production and there were lots more models and make-up artists milling around and I was completely out of my depth. I pretended to know what I was doing but I didn't have a clue and I just waited for people to tell me where I needed to be and when.

There was loads of champagne everywhere, which obviously I loved, but no food whatsoever. One of the other models asked if she could get some food and she was given a really funny look as if it was a ridiculous thing to ask. One girl I sat next to in the make up chair next to me had brought her own sandwich with her. I thought that was really sensible as we were booked to be there all day. But when I turned around to speak to her I realised that she was chewing the sandwich and then spitting it out into a tissue. I was really shocked and as I've never been known for my tact I blurted out, 'What on earth are you doing?' She smiled weakly and replied, 'Oh, I only wanted to taste it.' Of course she was scared about putting on weight. It was crazy.

I'd never walked down a catwalk before and I was petrified of falling over, so needless to say I drank quite a lot beforehand to make myself feel better. It helped me to forget how out of place I was feeling, and I remember thinking afterwards how different the world of modelling is to the world of athletics. Everyone in the modelling industry is so pretentious and full of themselves, and in my mind they hadn't actually achieved anything. At least in sports you're working hard and proving yourself. Still, I had to put those thoughts to the back of my mind. I had made the decision that being a model was what I was going to do and I had to try and make it work. I didn't really have much choice.

I kept hoping that the modelling work would increase and I would start making some proper money, but because I wasn't very established the agency kept putting me forward to do shows for new designers that paid next to nothing, or for unpaid jobs which were meant to help me to 'build up my portfolio'. Every model has to have a portfolio of pictures that they take around with them on castings so people can see how well they photograph. Mine was almost bare and it wasn't unusual for people who were new to the industry to do shoots and shows for free so that they could get a nice picture for their portfolio in return. I could kind of understand how it worked as it was a bit of a chicken and egg situation, but it wasn't like I had any savings to fall back on. I did do quite a few shows for free, but then it got to the point where I simply couldn't afford to do it any more, no matter how nice a picture they were going to give me at the end of it.

I needed money, and quickly. It had reached the point where I'd missed so many shifts at the pub that I'd had to quit. I was now completely broke and feeling quite desperate. I had about £400 to my name and there was no way I was going to ask my parents to lend me any cash. I had made the decision to move to London and I didn't want them to think that I needed their help in any way.

I was feeling a bit down and a friend of mine called Sarah, a fellow model, said her agency was having this big party at the Grosvenor House Hotel in Central London. She invited me along to cheer me up and it sounded like just what I needed. It was such a beautiful place and the whole event seemed really glamorous. Most of the people there were either models, fashion designers or they worked at the model agency, so it was a really cool, good-looking crowd. I felt good, it was amazing being there. This was the kind of party I could tell people in Wales about to prove that I had well and truly cracked London. In my eyes, this meant that I had made it.

The girls were all wearing what looked like really expensive dresses and I felt really envious. I'd used some of the last of my money to buy a long, backless pink dress from Karen Millen and I felt pretty good, but I also wished that I could afford the kind of outfits the other girls were wearing. I realise now that most of the dresses were probably on loan and they had to hand them back to the designers the next day.

All the drinks were completely free – anything you wanted – and loads of people were sitting around on these big, comfortable sofas looking fabulous. I remember this really famous Italian designer being there and he really reminded me of Hugh Heffner because he looked really old but he was surrounded by loads of young girls hanging off every word he said.

There was also a famous French fashion designer there, who was sitting on a table surrounded by all these girls. They had bottle after bottle of champagne cluttering up the table, and there was lots of laughter and flirting. It was no secret in the modelling world that the key to getting jobs was often about who you knew, which was why models were always so keen to get in with the designers.

Everyone at the party was there to get noticed and Sarah advised me to keep walking past the French designer to see if I could get invited to join him on his table. After the amount of champagne I'd drunk it seemed like a fantastic idea.

I must have walked past the table about three times before he eventually walked over to me and asked me if I wanted to join him. I followed him over and joined the six other girls sitting there, and we all sat there listening to what he was saying and pretending to be interested, when really he was boring the hell out of us. He basically just talked about himself for about half an hour and I laughed in all the right places while greedily tucking into the champagne.

I noticed that the other girls kept getting up and going to the toilet all the time, and at first I didn't realise what was going on. Then the girl who was sitting next to me came back sniffing from the toilet and suddenly I wised up to it. I had never touched drugs before – I'd never even smoked a joint – but I wasn't completely stupid and I could tell that all of these girls were probably on something; drugs were rife in that world.

I don't know what made me do it – whether it was because I wanted to fit in or just because I was so bored of this designer droning on – but I turned to the sniffing girl and smiled, 'Come on then, share what you've got!' Ten minutes later we slipped out to the toilet and went into a cubicle together. She got out a clear bag containing what looked like a tiny amount of white powder, but what I now know to be about two grams of cocaine.

She tipped a little pile onto the toilet cistern and then got out her credit card and started chopping the powder into two lines. She asked me if I'd ever done coke before and when I said no she grinned at me. She handed me a rolled up £20 note and I sucked one line up my left nostril and the other up my right. It was only afterwards that I realised one of the lines was supposed to be for her.

We went and sat back down and I suddenly got really panicky thinking, 'What if I die?' I expected to get a massive high from the coke or hallucinate or something, but I really didn't feel much and I was so disappointed. All it did was make me talk a lot. I literally couldn't stop and I was babbling on to anyone who would listen. I had a really dry mouth so I was drinking loads more champagne, but in a weird way the coke helped to sober me up.

Once I'd had those two lines I got a taste for it and I really wanted some more, so I asked the girl for another line. After that we were in the toilet all night together and we got through the entire two grams. By the end of the evening, if all the toilets were full, we were openly snorting it on the side of the sink. No one batted an eyelid, it was as if it was the most normal thing in the world.

I won't lie, I had an absolutely brilliant night. It felt like we were all one big, happy group sitting at that table, and all of a sudden I had all these amazing new mates who were totally on my wavelength. I even exchanged numbers with several people, although I never did speak to any of them again.

At the end of the evening the French designer went upstairs to a hotel room with all of the other girls and invited me to go along. The others had all been kissing him and fawning all over him and it all made me feel a bit ill. I kind of knew what they were going to get up to and it just wasn't my scene. I'd heard about designers taking advantage of young girls in those kinds of situations and it all felt very wrong. Despite being totally out of it, I knew I didn't want to be a part of that.

At about 5am I went outside and hailed a black cab. I literally slumped in the back seat exhausted, desperate for my bed. Of course when I got home and tried to go to sleep it was completely impossible. I was totally buzzing from the coke and I lay there with my eyes wide open. In the end I downed a load of vodka, enough to completely knock me out, and fell fast asleep.

I didn't wake up until early afternoon the next day and I felt like I'd been hit on the head with a brick. My solution? Drink some more vodka. I felt really jumpy and every time a car door slammed or I heard someone speaking outside I got all panicky. I knew I had to speak to my mum later that day and I got myself in a real state about it, thinking that somehow she would be able to tell that I'd taken drugs.

At about four o'clock I managed to make it to the local coffee shop to get some food. Even though I felt sick the sensible part of me knew that I had to eat in order to try and feel better. I sat at a table on my own and everyone was looking at me, probably because I looked a total state. My hair was all over the place and I still had some of my make up on from the night before. I ordered this big plate of food but when it arrived I pushed it away and I didn't eat a thing. I just couldn't face it.

For some reason Carl was on my mind a lot around this time. In spite of everything he had done to me, incredibly whenever I was feeling a bit fragile part of me still missed him. I thought if I could just see him one more time it might help me to have some 'closure'. Or maybe he would have changed and we could try and work things out between us? I texted him a picture of me that had been taken on one of my lingerie modelling shoots to see what he would say, and he texted me back immediately full of compliments. He said he'd been thinking about me and that he wanted to meet up and I felt my heart soar.

He came over to my place the next day and he was still every bit as gorgeous as I'd remembered. He told me that he was now totally single apart from dating a few girls here and there. He even showed me photos of one girl, a blonde, that he had been dating on and off. He told me that he wanted to be with me and he was going to dump her and all these other girls he had been seeing and go out with me exclusively. Although I didn't trust him, a small part of me felt a hint of excitement that maybe, just maybe, he was a different kind of person now.

I wanted to know for sure that I could trust him so I got a friend of mine who was a journalist and had access to the electoral roll to check out who he was living with. I can't say I was exactly shocked when she came back and said that he was still living with the same girlfriend as before. What did I expect? A leopard never changes its spots. I texted him and told him that I knew he was with her and I also threatened to tell her about me and all the other girls he had been seeing behind her back. I was all poised to do it when I stopped and thought. She knew what he was like and she had stayed with him all that time even though he had two-timed her so she wasn't helping herself, so what would be the point in telling her about his latest flings?

I was still livid with him, and I decided to get my revenge in the best way I could think of. I called up a celebrity magazine and told them that I had a story about a well-known rugby player and it was all theirs if they wanted it. I didn't want him to get away with doing what he'd done to me. People deserved to know the truth about him. The magazine was really keen on the story so they set up an interview between me and one of their features team. It seemed weird telling a total stranger the ins and outs of my life. Some of what I told her I'd never told anyone but it also felt good to get it out in the open. He had asked for it.

The article came out a few months later and it detailed exactly what he'd done to me. I got an abusive phone call from him, which I was fully expecting, but I told him calmly that what goes around comes around, and maybe next time he would think twice about treating someone so appallingly.

Carl was understandably furious and he started bad-mouthing me to people in the rugby world. He even started telling some of them that he had an injunction out against me as if I'd been stalking him or something. It was all completely ridiculous and I just laughed it off. I know it's not something everyone would do in order to get revenge but I will never regret giving that story to the magazine because it may just stop someone else getting involved with him.

Chapter 9

A MODEL LIFE

I felt jittery and sick for a couple of days following my first ever coke binge, but I certainly didn't let that put me off. When I went to see my hairdresser Peter a few days later I told him all about my big night out and what I'd done and he said, 'Oh babe, I do coke all the time. I can get you some if you want?' I'd finally been paid from a few modelling jobs I'd done so I handed over £100 there and then.

He went off for half an hour and came back with two grams for me and two grams for him, and we went back to his flat and did the lot. We sat up all night listening to cheesy music and smoking while I put £100 of drugs up my nose. At one point I started to feel really unwell and I was sick out of Peter's window. He laughed at me and said, 'Oh God babe, don't die on me will you?' I just smiled, shook my head and did another line.

I didn't leave Peter's until eight the next morning and then I did my old routine of going home, drinking and falling asleep. I woke up feeling like hell and all I could think about was having another line. I didn't give the fact that I was doing coke a second thought. From what I could see everyone in London was doing it and it felt like I was the only person on the party scene who hadn't been.

As time went on I got more and more into clubbing and got to know loads of people who went to the same places as me. Peter often came with me and we were like a dynamite duo going out in search of fun. Different clubs hosted different kinds of nights, and there was almost like a routine that people followed. Movida on a Tuesday, Paper on a Wednesday, and so on. I was going out most nights and taking coke and drinking, using the little bits of money that modelling was bringing in to get by. I was getting shows more frequently and a few paid £400 a time, so it finally seemed as if I was getting somewhere. However, I was very aware that if I wanted to keep going out all the time I was going to need a lot more money. Freddie's didn't seem to be doing a lot for me and so I decided to try my luck with some other agencies.

I sent all the modelling pictures I had so far off to several agencies, including a glamour agency. The owner Jenny sent me back a standard letter saying that I wasn't right for her agency, as did several of the others I wrote off to.

I knew that the glamour agency didn't just deal in modelling. A friend of mine was signed to them and she told me that they were often involved in selling kiss and tell stories to the tabloids. I emailed Jenny and said that I also had a kiss and tell that I could potentially sell for quite a bit of money. She was literally on the phone within minutes, called me 'darling' and 'babe' as if she was my best friend. She clearly had pound signs flashing before her eyes when she got my email and wanted to find out what I had to offer.

I had only ever sold that one story on Carl before and I had never planned to do it again, but desperate times called for desperate measures. In my alcohol and drug hazed state making a lot of money from the papers just for speaking to someone for a couple of hours sounded like a very good idea indeed.

I explained to Jenny that I'd been out with Gavin Henson, and as he had recently started dating the singer Charlotte Church, he was getting very well known. Journalists had already been to my parents' house looking for me because the British Lions tour was due to kick off and they were looking for a story on Gavin, so I knew I would be able to sell it no problem. And potentially make a good amount of money.

Jenny couldn't have sounded happier when I told her a few details about mine and Gavin's relationship and she asked me to go in to the agency and meet her. As soon as I got there she was all over me telling me that I had real potential as a model and a really great editorial look. Considering she'd turned me down saying I wasn't right for her agency the previous week that should really have set alarm bells ringing in my head. But I wanted to believe what she said when she told me she could get me loads of lucrative work, so I went along with it and agreed to let her sell the story.

Within two hours she called me back saying, 'The Sunday People and the News Of The World are interested. We're up to £15,000.' I was stunned. That was such a massive amount of money but I still didn't know if I could go through with it. I phoned my mum to ask her advice and of course she told me she didn't think it was a good idea and she tried to talk me out of it. But the more I thought about what a difference the money could make to my life, the more tempted I became. I put down the phone to my mum, cracked open a bottle of wine and after an hour I had made a firm decision – I was going to do it.

I had no idea how those things worked so I let Jenny deal with the newspaper side of things and she just told me where I needed to be and when. She set up a meeting with a journalist from The Sunday People and as it all happened really quickly I didn't have much time to think about the implications of doing something like that. It was only when I was in the cab on the way to the agency to do the interview that I realised what a big impact it could have on several people's lives. For a few minutes I wrestled with the idea of turning my phone off and asking the cab to turn around and drive me back home. But I was so desperate for the money that I couldn't see that I had any other option but to go through with it. My rent was due and I had no way of paying it. All my money from my recent modelling work had been snorted up my nose.

The interview was over pretty quickly, and it was only after I'd walked away I realised how much I had revealed. Journalists are so clever at getting stuff out of you that you don't mean to say, but I didn't think any of it would come across as seedy as mine and Gavin's relationship wasn't like that. We'd been young and it had all been pretty innocent so how bad could it be?

After the interview I went straight to a bar called Cheers on Regent Street in Central London. I sat on my own and proceeded to get very, very drunk. I felt really upset by the interview and the more I thought about the things that I had revealed the more panicky I felt. I had always been a very private person and I didn't really talk about relationships and things, so the fact that I was revealing intimate stuff about a past love? I was mortified.

I got completely legless and I phoned my friend

Simon who came to collect me. He could tell that I was plastered and it would have been dangerous for me to try and get home on my own. I was so drunk I was sick on the tube home, but by the time we reached Putney I was getting my second wind. We headed straight to a pub called The Blue Anchor, where we used to hang out, as I was desperate for another drink.

Simon had told everyone in the pub where I'd been and what I'd done that day, so when I walked in all the people I knew stood up and clapped and cheered. I laughed along, then ordered a large glass of wine and downed it in one. Then I stayed there for the rest of the night downing wine after wine.

I woke up the next morning with the worst hangover I've ever had and I immediately opened another bottle of wine to take the edge off. The journalist kept calling me to get some more details on some of the things I'd told her. I eventually took her call and she told me that the newspaper had also been trying to call Gavin to give him a right to reply which made me really angry. Of course he was going to find out about the story when it came out the following weekend, but I didn't want him involved at this stage.

He was already away on the British Lions tour but someone did eventually get hold of him and told him all about the story. He just snapped, 'Talk to my agent,' and put the phone down on them. I can't say I'm surprised. The journalist then called his agent and all he would say was, 'I can confirm that Gavin had a relationship with this woman. I have no further comment.' Oh dear.

I had to do a photo shoot to go with the story a few days later. I had to wear about five different outfits, and I just pretended to myself that it was another modelling photo shoot. I actually ended up having a lot of fun. The photographer, Martin, was really lovely and made me feel so comfortable. He was like a kindly uncle or something. We chatted for ages after the shoot and he even offered to help me find a new agent as I was having doubts about the glamour agency. Something about Jenny made me feel uneasy.

The night before the story was due to come out in the paper I was in the Blue Anchor and a woman from The People called me because she had to read the copy down the phone to me to make sure I was happy with it. Thankfully I had copy approval so I managed to get her to take a couple of the worst bits out, but it was still awful. The girl who had interviewed me had done a really good job, but the features editor had decided to add all this other stuff in because he already had an idea in his head of how the feature should read.

When it came to saying goodbye the woman from The People said cheerily to me, 'Well done, well done, it's a great story!' and I thought 'Well done for what? For selling a story on someone who is going to get really hurt by it? Yes, well done me.'

When the story came out the following day I got up early for once when my friend came round with a copy of the paper. I gasped when I saw it. The headline read: 'Gavin Henson is rubbish in the sack.' The story made him look so much worse than he actually is. They had included the story about how he'd dressed up as Elvis, but instead of making him look funny, it made him look stupid. Some of the other stuff made him sound really bad as well, and they took the mickey out of his hair and his tan and made out like he fancied himself far more than he fancied me. That may well have been true, but it wasn't what I'd told them.

My mum phoned me up and I was waiting for her to shout and get angry, but instead she told me that it was my choice but I was going to have to deal with the fallout from it, whatever that may be. Then she joked, 'The photo of you is nice, but you should have had your nails done.'

I didn't really hear from anyone else, I guess people were embarrassed and didn't really know what to say me. The worst thing was that Jenny didn't even call me to see if I was alright. She was going to get her money so she didn't really care how I was feeling. I think that has to be one of the loneliest days I've had. I felt very cut off from people and I was worried that everyone would think I was really cheap and that they'd want nothing to do with me. I didn't even want to leave the flat in case people recognised me.

The following morning I was watching GMTV when Lorraine Kelly came on and announced that Charlotte Church was going to be live on the show the following morning. I listened open mouthed as she said, 'Tomorrow Charlotte Church will be telling us how model Amy Bohan's recent revelations about her boyfriend Gavin Henson have no bearing on their relationship whatsoever.' I guess that made it all the more real and made me realise that of course people had read the story. Now people would know my name for all the wrong reasons.

I woke up early the next morning to find out what Charlotte had to say about me. I was worried that she would launch a verbal attack on me – and she would have been well within her rights – because she's known for her feisty nature. Instead she said, 'Well you can't blame these people, they get offered so much money.' She didn't mention my name or anything which I was really relieved about. Being in the paper was bad enough; I didn't want my name being bandied about on television as well.

I didn't hear from Jenny again until the following Thursday when she phoned me and asked if I wanted to be in The Sport. I didn't really know a lot about the paper but I knew it was quite sleazy, but when she said they were willing me pay me £1000 I thought 'Why not?' It was a lot more than all of the modelling jobs were paying me and the story was already out there so what was the harm in it? Then she dropped the bombshell that they wanted me to go topless. I laughed because my boobs were only 32b and I knew that The Sport usually used busty glamour girls, so I couldn't understand why they were interested in me.

I had never done topless shots before and I felt really nervous about it. I was crossing a line in a way, but I was only thinking about the money and how much alcohol and coke I could buy with it. Coke was getting to be quite a regular habit and it cost a lot of money, so I needed to pay for it somehow.

I eventually agreed to go topless and Jenny called me and told me to go to a studio near London Bridge. It looked really dodgy and it was scummy inside, but it still looked pretty professional. There were these two other girls already there who were also doing a shoot. Neither were terribly pretty but they had these huge boobs and again I thought 'Why on earth do they want me topless? You'll barely notice me next to these girls.'

When it was my turn to pose the photographer produced a rugby ball and asked me to pose with it. I just burst out laughing because it made my boobs look even smaller. But I thought it was so hilarious that I ended up doing it after a bit of persuasion.

Because I was doing quite a lot of coke and I'd been stressed I hadn't been eating an awful lot. As a result I had lost a lot of weight in the two weeks before the shoot so I didn't think I would look in any way sexy, and I was right. I wanted to cry when I saw the photos. I looked disgusting. But I had agreed for them to be used so I did my best to put it to the back of my mind and I didn't even buy the paper when it came out.

The Sport also asked me if I wanted to sit in front of a web cam topless and talk to their readers for an extra £100. I politely declined their offer. That really was a step too far.

Chapter 10

LOST IN LONDON

So much for me getting the money to pay my rent in time. I had to wait two months for any of the money to come through, and when I did eventually get paid I got about half what I expected to get for the main interview I did. I have no idea what happened to the rest of it or why it took so long for me to get the money because I know that The People paid the fee within a week. I also have no idea what happened to the money that I was supposed to be paid for the photo shoot that ran alongside the interview, or for the Sport piece. I never saw a penny of it.

Jenny also sold the story on to a news agency and to several tabloid columns but I didn't get paid for any of that either. Basically, I got totally ripped off. I know I shouldn't complain because it was still quite a lot of money, but I was upset that Jenny had taken advantage of me and I had been stupid enough to let her. I tried to chase her up on the other money I was owed but she was always really vague about it and said that she was chasing the newspapers who owed it to us. She always had some excuse.

Thankfully while I'd been waiting for the bulk of the money to be paid Peter had agreed to lend me some money. Most of it went on coke and soon my life started to spiral out of control. Not only was I drinking every day, but generally I was doing coke every day as well. I became really incoherent really quickly from being so high all the time, and several people I spoke to on the phone around that time later admitted to me that after they'd put down the phone to me they'd said to people, 'Amy sounds really weird these days, I wonder what's wrong with her?' No one thought to ask me if I was on drugs. If anything they just thought I was drunk as usual. I hid my coke-taking well.

The more drugs I did the more insecure I got. I was forever asking people if they genuinely liked me and if they were really my friend. I also virtually stopped eating altogether. If it was a choice between coke and food, coke won every time. To save money I used to buy a box of porridge and have it with water so I didn't have to buy milk as well. At one point I was pretty much living on coke, booze and porridge.

I went down to around seven and a half stone, and I looked absolutely tiny. I used to feel weak all the time and I also passed out several times. Everyone thinks that as a model the skinnier you are the more successful you are, but that's not the case if you've got black rings under your eyes and your skin looks grey. I looked horrendous. I just couldn't see it.

Jenny kept telling me that she would get me more newspaper interviews and she even offered to try and get me on some TV shows talking about Gavin, but I refused. She wanted to milk the story for all it was worth so that she could make more money, and I suspect she knew I had a drug problem and needed all the cash I could get.

Jenny set up another interview with The People without telling me, where I was supposed to reveal more stuff about Gavin. Without any warning she called me saying that I had to go and meet this journalist in a pub. She then instructed me not to say a word to the journalist unless they gave me cash first. It all sounded very dodgy, especially as I hadn't agreed to it, so I didn't turn up for the interview. I didn't have anything else to say about Gavin anyway, and I wasn't going to sit there and make up a pack of lies so she could rip me off again.

I was sick of Jenny and I knew she was no good for me, so I looked around for other agencies to sign with. Unfortunately none of the serious model agencies wanted anything to do with me after I'd done a kiss and tell. You're virtually blacklisted after you've done something like that, so I had effectively killed my modelling career there and then. I wish I'd thought and known more about the consequences before I did the story but I didn't know any better.

I ended up bumping into the journalist who interviewed me for The People about a year after the story came out. She admitted to me that when she was interviewing me she was thinking, 'This girl is so naïve. I hope someone is looking after her because she could end up in trouble.' But clearly no one was looking out for me. Hence things got worse and worse for me.

When I did finally get paid for the first People interview the first thing I did was go and get my hair done, and the second thing I did was buy a few grams of coke. It was good to know that I had a little stash to fall back on. I took it every time I went clubbing, which was a lot, so I knew I would always want it and it made sense to buy in bulk. All of a sudden I felt rich.

Peter and I decided that we were a bit bored of London and we fancied some real excitement. It felt as if we'd 'done' London in a way, as we'd been to every top club loads of times and we were well known on the scene. We wanted a new challenge and some new excitement, and now I had some cash to go and find it.

We wanted somewhere that was easy to get to,

extremely glamorous and full of hot men. Paris it was! It took no time to get there on the Eurostar so one night we headed down to Waterloo with a bottle of champagne and some cash in our pockets and got on the first train we could. We hadn't thought about the logistics of what we were going to do when we got there, we just wanted an adventure.

When we got off the Eurostar at Paris we looked at each other and laughed our heads off at how ridiculous it all seemed. We got a tram into the centre of Paris and went into the first bar we could find: a place called The Buddha Bar. We started asking people where we could go and which clubs were good. This one guy, who was a half English, half French man called Jean, recommended a club called Le Belle that he was going to. We were up for anything so when he offered to take us we said we'd go along with him. What he didn't tell us was that he owned the club.

It was a proper after hours place with pool tables and escort girls everywhere. It wasn't the kind of place you could just walk into off the street, you'd have to know someone just to get through the door. There was a dance floor filled with people, and drugs were readily available. Peter and I bought some coke and after a few lines we proceeded to dance the night away. Our first train back wasn't until seven in the morning so we needed to find a way to fill the time and dancing and doing drugs seemed like the best option.

After the club closed at around five loads of people piled back to Jean's apartment and he invited us back as well. Our train wasn't until seven in the morning and it seemed like a much better idea than sitting in a cold train station for two hours.

Jean's place was really strange. It was like he had two flats in one; the basement area was really seedy. It smelt like dirty money and there were condoms everywhere, while the upstairs area was really flashy with expensive furniture and oil paintings. It looked to me like the basement flat was used for prostitution or something and I didn't like the atmosphere down there at all.

Peter and I stayed in the upstairs flat snorting lines and drinking whatever was available. We looked around and suddenly realised that it was exactly like being back on the London party scene. Everyone was in their little cliques and everywhere you looked people were chopping out lines.

Peter and I ended up staying in the flat for three days in all, with no sleep, as people drifted in and out. Jean seemed happy to let people use his place to crash in and he had blackout blinds so even in the middle of the day it seemed like it was night time. Peter and I lost all track of time and every time we felt a bit tired we bought more drugs from someone at the party to pep us up.

It got to the point where we had to go home. It was getting a bit ridiculous and it was as if our lives were slowly ebbing away the longer we spent in the flat. We'd spent all of our money on drugs and we hadn't brought any bank cards with us, so thankfully Jean paid for our Eurostar tickets back to London. He was obviously absolutely loaded so it meant nothing to him but I have no idea what we would have done if he'd refused. But then, I kind of knew he wouldn't say no. He had obviously taken a shine to me and he spent most of the time we were there flirting with me.

We kissed before I left and Jean asked me to come back on my own and visit him. He flew me over and we started seeing each other quite regularly. Most weekends I would pack a small bag and head to the airport destined for Paris. I always flew first class and he spoilt me rotten. He was a multi-millionaire and owned a 96-foot boat that was worth six million pounds alone. He even flew to Milan from Paris one night just to have dinner. It was all quite crazy. He always took me for stupidly expensive meals and bought me Cristal champagne, and he appeared to have coke on tap. Everything was always so lavish. It was the first time I had properly dated anyone since Carl so it took me a while to trust him but he showered me with compliments and looked after me so well that I soon fell for him.

The fourth time I went to see him we went back to Le Belle to meet some of his friends. He had a few grams of coke so we went into his office to do some lines. I was snorting some off his desk when he opened the top drawer to get something out. I flicked my eyes down to the open drawer and the first thing I saw was a gun. I had never seen a real gun up close and it totally freaked me out. I was completely paranoid that he was going to do something to me so I started shouting at him and ran out of the club and down the road. He came after me and said it was nothing to do with him and that they'd found it in the club one night so he'd put it in the drawer to keep it safe. I was so out of it I kept shouting, 'You're going to kill me, you're going to kill me!' He managed to calm me down and took me back to his place. I felt like such an idiot when I woke up the next morning but neither of us mentioned what had happened.

Through Jean I met a French model agent during one of my visits to Paris. He ran a commercial agency and he said that he thought I could do very well over there. I was excited about the prospect of moving to Paris and catwalk shows, but when I got back to London and told another model about what the agent had said she claimed that to get any jobs in Paris I would have to sleep with the casting agents and photographers. It may have been a case of sour grapes but I was already so paranoid that needless to say it put me off working over there. Every time the French agency called and asked me to go and see them I knocked them back. It's a shame because it would have been interesting to see what had happened over there and if I really could have made it, but it's one of those things I will never know.

The next time I went to see Jean I took a friend with me called Holly, who I had met on the London party scene. We were in Le Belle dancing when Jean rushed up to us and said we had to get out immediately. One of club bouncers took us to Jean's place and then sat outside in a car for hours watching the flat. We didn't have any drugs or cigarettes so I tried to sneak out to buy some cigarettes, but as soon as the bouncer saw me he ran over and angrily told me to get back inside.

I wasn't stupid, I knew there was lots of dodgy stuff going on with Jean, but at first I thought it was quite a buzz. I heard all sorts of rumours about him being involved in dodgy dealings, but I thought it was all blown out of proportion. But after that night I began to feel more and more uneasy about everything.

The last time I ever went to visit Jean I went on my own and I headed straight to Le Belle to meet him. I couldn't find him anywhere, so I went to his office and I walked in to find him standing there with some terrified looking guy pinned to the wall. One of the bouncers was standing nearby menacingly and when the bouncer spotted me he pushed me out of the room and told me that Jean was having a 'meeting'. It wasn't like any kind of meeting I'd ever seen. It had all seemed quite funny before but when I saw what looked like someone about to be hurt it made me wake up a bit and realise that I was way out of my depth.

Jean and my relationship petered out but I stayed in touch with him and we're still friends. I spoke to him just last year, but I won't be going back to Le Belle anytime soon. I sometimes find it hard to breathe when I think about it now and I often wonder what really went on there.

Chapter 11

CHAMPAGNE CHARLIE

I knew that the money I had made from selling the story on Gavin Henson wouldn't last forever and I needed to think about what I was going to do to get by in the future. Several people had made it clear to me that now I'd done a kiss and tell there was no way I was going to get mainstream modelling work, so I thought the next best thing would be glamour modelling. I wasn't about to go all out and do anything too revealing, but I had already done a topless shoot so my attitude was, 'What the hell? Why not do more?'

I couldn't see what else I was going to do job-wise that would allow me to keep up my current lifestyle, and modelling meant that I was accepted on the London party scene – something I was still desperate to be a part of.

Martin, the guy who did the shoot for The People for me, agreed to take some shots so I could build up a glamour portfolio. I posed for some topless pictures and also some very tasteful naked shots. I was really pleased with them and it gave my confidence a real boost. I was still very skinny at that time but somehow Martin made the shots look amazing. I guess it was partly to do with the camera putting weight on you. I doubt many models have been pleased about that happening before, but for me it was a Godsend.

Martin suggested that instead of trying to sign with one of the big modelling agencies I go with lots of small ones so I had more chance of getting work. That way several different people would be sending me out for castings at the same time, which would hopefully keep me busy.

I approached three agencies initially and they all said they would put me on their books on the strength of the shots I'd had done. I also asked them to try and get me fashion work as well as glamour if at all possible, and I was all geared up to make a real go of things. I even managed to cut back on the drugs and drinking a bit, but then the constant scrutiny and criticism on the castings soon began to get me down again. The days were so long and it was so demoralising. I would go to ten castings on a day and get one job if I was lucky.

One small fashion agency, Beat, were great because they got me lots of work in lingerie fashion shows so I did at least start getting some money in, but sometimes I got so down that instead of going to castings I would go and sit in a pub and drink all day on my own. That got worse when I found out there was a way I could get work without actually going to the castings.

When I went for jobs for the bigger fashion houses the casting people would take a Polaroid of you so they could remember the models when deciding who to book. However, the jobs I was going to now were so unorganised that they didn't bother to take a photo of you. In fact, they didn't even take your name. Beat used to call me and say, 'Did you go the casting today?' and when I said yes they'd say, 'Great, because the designer wants to cast all the Beat girls who went to the casting in the fashion show.' So I'd turn up at the show and no one would be any the wiser. No one could remember who had gone to the casting and who hadn't, so I'd just roll up and get on with it.

That meant that I could get away with sitting in pubs and only leaving when I had a show to do. I did a lot of smaller catwalk shows and I thought because they weren't as big as other fashion shows I'd done they wouldn't be as bitchy, but I was wrong. And they weren't nearly as much fun as the ones I used to do. There was no champagne and you weren't even allowed fizzy drinks because they bloat you out. If you were there all day all you'd get for lunch was salad and still water. Mind you, at least we got *some* food I guess. The minute the shows were over I'd always head straight to the bar and drink away all my annoyance at how we were treated.

I soon realised how boring the shows could be so Peter started coming along with me when he wasn't working. He'd drive me and we'd get some coke and have a laugh anyway. At the Lingerie shows the girls always had bigger boobs than me and they didn't mind getting naked in front of everyone, but I was much more self-conscious at first. I was always a little shy and I wished my 32A boobs were bigger so I'd kind of hide when I got changed. Modelling is very good at making you feel inadequate because if you don't get a certain job you wonder why, and I know that a lot of the girls that did lingerie shows had similar hang ups to me. However, as time went on I got more confident about how I looked. It was Peter who made me feel better by saying that boob size doesn't make anyone any worse or any better than anyone else, and of course he was right. After that I'd strip off in front of anyone. Everyone else did it and it became the norm.

I carried on doing my trick of skipping castings and then turning up for jobs for another couple of months or so, but I got found out after this one girl worked out that I hadn't been going to the castings but I had been doing the jobs. She was furious. She started crying and was almost screaming with anger backstage at one of the shows, and she told the boss of the company what I'd been up to. Not surprisingly I got sacked immediately.

I was still signed to the other agencies but I wasn't getting as much work from them so it was a big blow, but of course it was my own stupid fault. What did I expect? I was bound to get caught out at some point, I just wish it had been several months later when I had managed to make some decent money.

The fact that I had less work on meant that I was far more free to do drugs and I was getting into a routine of doing a few lines of coke just to get me up in the morning. I was quite enjoying being wild and in a weird way I thought this was what moving to London was all about. I assumed that everyone else was doing just as many drugs as me. They were so easy to get hold of I almost felt like I was *supposed* to be doing them. I was offered them every time I went out and I already knew a few dealers so getting a few grams was as easy as ordering a pizza.

I still had some of the money I was paid for the Gavin Henson story and despite not doing much modelling work at that time, I was throwing it around all over the place. I didn't invest any of it. Not one single penny. To me it was just play money. I would happily buy bottles of champagne on a night out and I thought nothing of spending £150 in one go on coke.

At that time I was mainly getting the drugs from a guy who hung out in one of the pubs where I used to work. It wasn't as if I was having to go to some dodgy drugs den on a seedy estate to score, I'd just pop up to my local and hand over the cash.

I was still very dependent on alcohol having to drink more and more to get any effect from it. Soon my morning line started being accompanied by a glass or two of wine. It was the norm for me to wake up, open a bottle of wine and chop out a line of coke just to get me going. I don't how I didn't stop and look at what I was doing at any point and think about the long-term effects. I guess I was just on a roll and I couldn't have stopped even if I'd wanted to.

The thing that really upsets me is that no one reigned me in. I didn't have many real friends at the time – just the people I used to go partying with – and they didn't care that I was in a bit of a state because they were probably just as bad as me. And of course, if they pointed out that I had a problem they would then have to take a look at themselves.

I wish just one person had taken me aside and told me to sort myself out or try and get me help. But instead people were using me. Instead of suggesting that I go to rehab they were sharing my coke. And rather than suggest that I don't have any more to drink on a night out, they'd buy me a double vodka. It was all about how far you could push things and how much fun you could have. There was almost an intimacy and respect between people who could really go the distance. But in retrospect, I really wasn't having much fun at all.

I went to see some more agencies at the height of my addiction in a bid to get more work but most of them just looked me up and down and told me a firm no. I did go and see this one agency called M&P and the girl in there was so sweet and said to me, 'You're very pretty but you look really poorly and really ill. I don't want to speak out of turn but I'm concerned that you have some kind of drug problem. Maybe come back when you're better.' She gave me a kiss on the cheek and recommended that I went and got some counselling. But she was the only one out of all the agencies I visited who was nice to me. All the others treated me like I was trash and turned their noses up at me.

If only I had listened to the girl from M&P's advice and gone and got counselling I may not have gone on to become even more of a mess. I was drinking at every opportunity and I had a drink in my hand practically the entire time I was at home. When I wasn't at home I was in a pub somewhere sitting on my own at a bar talking to complete strangers, or I was out partying and getting smashed.

One day I got asked to go on some castings by one of the two agencies who would still deal with me. They were due to start at ten in the morning and go on until around six and that was a major problem for me. I would have no way of having a drink if I needed one. The thought really panicked me, so I decanted vodka into a water bottle and carried it around with me so I could take sips during the day. After that I carried a 'water bottle' with me at all times.

Even if I went shopping I'd walk around the shops on Oxford Street drinking vodka from the bottle. I thought I was so clever because no one had clue what I was doing. People who saw me must have thought that something was up with me though. I thought I hid my problem so well but I was so hammered all the time I was probably staggering. I'll never forget coming out of Oasis on Argyll Street, which is right next to Oxford Circus, and throwing up on the street because I was so wasted. That's one of the lowest points of my life but – and I think you know what's coming – it didn't put me off drinking one bit.

My family had absolutely no idea what was going on with me. As far as they were concerned I was still happily living in London carving out a career for myself as a model and making a success of my life. I hadn't spoken to them for ages, which was all my doing.

As soon as I started doing coke in June 2005 I knew that I needed to cut all ties with them in case they found out what I was doing and tried to stop me, so I started a stupid argument with my mum on the phone one day, and managed to cause a huge fall out. After that I changed my phone number so they couldn't get hold of me.

I was so manipulative and even though in some ways I was desperate for someone to help me, the selfish, stupid part of me didn't want anyone or anything to get in the way of my partying. I was 22 and I thought I was perfectly capable of standing on my own two feet and I didn't need anyone telling me what to do.

My parents still sent me a birthday card the following September and they also sent me some money so I could buy myself something nice, but I'm very ashamed to say that it went straight on coke. I suppose at the time that *was* my idea of buying something nice.

Chapter 12

HEY, MR DJ...

Around October 2005 I met a guy called Fraser in Chinawhite. He had initially started chatting up a friend of mine while I was in the toilets doing some coke, but then when I came back he turned his attentions to me. What a charmer!

He bought us some really expensive cocktails, and then later as I walked past the DJ booth I saw him standing in there. I was quite out of it so I started shouting, 'Get out of there! What are you doing? That's where the DJ should be!' He shouted back, 'I'm working. I am the DJ!' I have to admit, I was impressed. DJs are always considered to be some of the coolest people on the club scene, and he also happened to DJ in my favourite club.

I didn't fancy Fraser at first but he seemed like a nice guy and I thought it wouldn't hurt to have a bit of fun. So when he asked me out I said yes. My mate wasn't interested in him so she told me to go for it.

We ended up seeing each other for a couple of months and if I'm being honest, a big part of the reason I stayed with him was because he could get me into all the clubs for free. There were still a few I had to pay for and some of them were about £20 a pop, which was more money I could have been spending on coke.

I loved the fact that I could wander up to certain clubs and know that I was on the guest list. But after a while Fraser started to get really funny with me because I think he could tell I wasn't that into him. I just didn't like him in that way. I liked his company and I thought he was quite cute so I was happy to snog him, but I didn't want to sleep with him just for the sake of it.

I knew Fraser and I didn't have any future together but we got on well so I think we stayed with each other simply because we had a laugh. He was always on coke as well so we weren't exactly good together as we encouraged each other, but we had a good time and we were more like good mates than anything else.

One night I was in the VIP area of Chinawhite on my own. I was supposed to be meeting Fraser but he'd got his shifts mixed up and he was DJ-ing in the late slot instead of the early one, so he couldn't come and see me, so I was left all alone. I was quite annoyed about it and it obviously showed on my face. For once there was no one else I knew in there and so I sat there moodily drinking my wine.

There was this really posh man sitting opposite me wearing a really smart suit. He was talking to Sid Owen from EastEnders and I could tell they were talking about me. The next thing I knew the guy in the suit leaned over and asked me what was wrong. I guess it must have been pretty obvious I was in a mood! He seemed genuinely concerned that I was on my own. I told him that I'd been stood up and that no one would dance with me. He smiled and announced in this grand posh voice, 'Darling, *I'll* dance with you.'

He seemed like a laugh so we went off for a dance, much to the annoyance of Fraser who was watching us from the DJ booth. The man in the suit and I spent the rest of the night chatting and he told me all about himself. He was called Edward and he was a well respected businessman and he was such a lovely bloke. I found him so easy to talk to and even though he was quite a bit older than me at 42, there was something about him I was hugely attracted to. We couldn't have been more different though. He was so well spoken and gentle, and while I was swearing every other word, he'd say things like 'Oops a daisy.'

Fraser and I were going on to a party, so when the time came to leave I decided to go for it and I asked for Edward's number. He handed over his business card and as I was going out the door I texted him saying how nice it was to meet him, and that I hoped I would see him again. He texted straight back but then I didn't hear anything for a couple of days so I was really disappointed. I decided that if he wanted to see me again it was up to him to get in touch as I had made the first move. I needed to be confident that he liked me back.

He eventually left me a message four days after we'd first met saying, 'Hello, it's Edward here. I think I had a dance or two with you on the weekend. Give me a call back if you get a minute.' It took me a while to pluck up the courage to call him, and I only felt confident enough to do it once I'd had a couple of lines. I even did a line while I was on the phone to him because I felt so jittery about speaking to him.

It was very clear that Fraser and I weren't a match made in heaven and we were going nowhere relationship wise, but I couldn't bring myself to have the 'I think we should split up' conversation with him. In the meantime Edward and I were talking quite regularly, and we arranged to meet up. He took me out for dinner to a lovely, quiet little restaurant in Soho and he was so lovely to me. He didn't try anything on and we had a really nice evening.

Fraser had invited me to this big private party he was DJ-ing at, so I took Edward along with me.

Even though nothing was ever said about it Fraser definitely got the message that we were well and truly over that night and our relationship – if you can call it that – very naturally turned into a friendship.

Edward and I started seeing a lot more of each other in the run up to Christmas. He treated me so well and I always felt so comfortable around him. Although I was still drinking a hell of a lot I toned down the drugs because for the first time in ages I felt like I had something in my life that was really good. Edward was always quite hyperactive so I had assumed he did coke as well, but when he told me that he didn't touch drugs it gave me the incentive to cut down as well. As far as he was concerned I didn't do any at all, so I felt like it was best to calm things down as much as possible. I wouldn't be surprised if he could tell I was on drugs anyway though. I was still very skinny and I always had big bags under my eyes that I tried to hide with lots of make up. But then, I was a model. And didn't most models look like that, drugs or not?

I hadn't spoken to my parents for months but when Christmas came around I started to feel sad and I missed my family. I knew that staying in London on my own for Christmas would make me feel really depressed, but equally I didn't know how on earth I could go back home to Wales? How would I be able to drink constantly? And what if someone worked out that I was doing drugs?

I mulled it over for days and decided that I'd go home for a few days so that I could see my parents and my brother. I knew it would mean a lot to my mum and dad to see me, and if I'm being honest, what I wanted more than anything was a hug from my mum. I called home and my mum was so pleased to hear from me she cried. That was when I knew for certain I was doing the right thing.

I had bought an old car with some of the money I had been paid by The People, and on Christmas Eve I loaded up the car, did a couple of lines of coke and set off up the M4. I wore sunglasses the whole way even thought it was dark because I felt quite paranoid and the bright lights of the other cars hurt my eyes. I must have looked like a right lunatic zooming down the motorway in the pitch black wearing a huge pair of shades.

When I walked through the door of my family home everyone looked at me as if I was a total stranger. The last time they had seen me I had looked relatively healthy, but here I was looking skinny, tired, drawn and wearing a ridiculous outfit that consisted of a summer dress, knee high boots and a cardigan.

My brother told me later that my clothes were the thing he noticed first because nothing matched and it looked like I had picked up whatever was on my bedroom floor and thrown the lot on. Which, to be fair, was probably what I had done. My brother went straight to my parents and told them that he thought I was doing drugs, but of course it wasn't something they wanted to hear. They could see that I was in a mess, but every time they tried to talk to me about it I would shout and scream. When my brother confronted me I got really angry and started shouting, 'How dare you accuse me of being on drugs! Do you want mum and dad to know about all the things you've got up to in the past?' He left me alone after that.

I only went out once while I was back in Wales. I ventured into town with my old friend Richard on Christmas Eve, and as we were walking through St Mary's arcade in Cardiff I saw this girl I recognised. It took a few seconds for me to register that it was Charlotte Church. She spotted me immediately and started shouting all kinds of names at me. She didn't seem to care who heard. Her friends had to hold her back because it looked like she was going to throw herself at me and start hitting me, and I immediately turned around and walked the other way. I wasn't scared of her but she was making a real scene, and be honest I was more embarrassed for her than anything. I could still hear her shouting after me as I walked away but I just kept going. What would be the point in standing up to her and making things worse? At least she'd got to have her say. In a way I really hope that made her feel better because what I did must have been very hurtful. The things I said aren't the kind of things that I would want to read about my boyfriend in the newspaper.

Christmas day itself was nice and went pretty smoothly. Because I had only decided to go down to Wales at the last minute my present shopping was done in about half an hour and I'd bought some strange gifts. I'd got my parents some random books as it was quick and easy, and I got my brother a lot of sex paraphernalia, which he opened in front of my parents. God knows what I was thinking. I must have been off my head to do that but I laughed my head off when I saw how red he went. I was drunk. For a change.

I only managed to stay in Wales for two days before I started to feel like I was going a bit crazy. Somehow I stayed off the coke while I was there and that made me feel really grumpy and I was aware that I was very snappy with people. I had taken two bottles of vodka down with me so I was sneaking off and drinking that constantly, and I also drank a whole bottle of Baileys once the vodka ran out. I felt so sick, but I couldn't stop myself from finishing the lot.

My parents kept trying to subtly question me about my lifestyle and what I had been doing in London, but I didn't want to answer any of their questions. Of course they were only trying to help but it just sounded like a load of annoying noise in my head. I kept shouting at them to back off and in the end on Boxing Day I packed up my things and drove back to London. I knew I had coke waiting for me back at the flat and I wanted to go partying and escape from what I saw as an inter-rogation.

When New Year rolled around I was determined to go out and have a good time and forget about everything that had happened when I'd been back home. Edward and I had been speaking on the phone quite a lot and I was starting to like him more and more. We hadn't even kissed but I was hopeful that something would happen between us.

I knew from some of the things he'd said to me that he liked me too, so when he asked me to go out with him on New Year's Eve I viewed it as our first proper date. We decided that just the two of us would go out and if we bumped into anyone else we knew, then so be it, but we wouldn't actually arrange to meet anyone as such.

I went to Edward's house first and drank a bottle of champagne between us, and then we went to a club over near Buckingham Palace. It was absolutely crap. It was horribly busy and it had no atmosphere, so after a couple of hours we decided to move on to Chinawhite. We had some more drinks and then I slipped off to the bathroom to do some coke. Edward still had no idea that I did so I had to be really subtle about it.

We were both keen to spend time together without too many interruptions so we hardly spoke to anyone else all night. People who saw us together would definitely have thought we were a couple. We were really affectionate with each other and we laughed constantly. I felt totally comfortable in his company and I trusted him one hundred percent, which was a very rare thing for me.

We were having a great time and we were dancing like crazy, and I soon totally forgot about the hideousness of Christmas. I was completely hammered and I decided to make the night that bit more enjoyable with another line. I was worried that all the alcohol I'd had would make me sleepy so I headed to the toilet. I stood in a queue for ages and as soon as a cubicle came free I dived in. I sat down on the toilet for a minute to rest before I chopped out my line and the next thing I knew I woke up three hours later still in the same position with the toilet attendant shouting, 'Lady, wake up! Wake up!' at me. I had a total panic and checked my phone to find five missed calls and several text messages from a very worried Edward wondering where the hell I was.

I stumbled out into the club to find him but it was clearing out and he was nowhere to be seen. I felt really weary so I texted Edward to let him know that I was okay and then jumped into a cab and went home to bed. So much for our amazing first date. I thought I'd bagged myself a really nice guy but I'd managed to totally mess it up. Typical me.

When I woke up the next day my head was throbbing, but more than anything I felt massively disappointed in myself. It had been my big chance to impress Edward and I'd ruined everything. I didn't think I'd ever hear from him so I was so happy when he sent me a text message to check if I was okay. I thought it was best to be honest with him so I texted back: 'I'm so sorry. I was so drunk I fell asleep in the toilet cubicle.' Thankfully he saw the funny side and texted back, 'Such a shame. You looked so elegant when you went out as well!' I had been wearing this lovely Karen Millen dress and some black shoes from Ted Baker and I had felt great. I suspect I didn't look quite as good at the end of the evening.

New Year's Day felt like a bit of a wake up call for me. I think as it does with a lot of people, the start of the New Year made me reevaluate my life and take a step back from everything. And what did I have? A drug and alcohol problem, a modelling career I was struggling to keep going, a bank balance that was dwindling rapidly thanks to my ridiculous spending, and no real friends to speak of, apart from Edward. And it was entirely possible that I'd jeopardized that as well.

I sat in my bed staring at the wall and wondered how the hell things had gone so wrong? In six months I had gone from someone who was excited about moving to London and what the future held, to a messed up girl who couldn't even get out of bed in the morning without the help of some form of chemical. It seems crazy now but back then I saw drugs as a way to make friends and bond with people. I had ultimately given myself an addiction to make friends.

I started crying and once I started I found I couldn't stop. I sobbed until my chest hurt and I felt weak. I had well and truly fucked everything up and I had no one to blame but myself. Then I did the only thing that I knew would make me feel better. I went to the pub.

Thankfully Edward eventually forgave me for the New Year's incident and we started seeing each other properly around the middle of January. He instantly had a really calming effect on me and I decided that I wanted to really make a go of things with him. He had no idea that I was doing drugs and I was worried that if he found out he wouldn't want anything to do with me, so I decided to try and stop taking the coke completely. I cut down slowly and it wasn't easy but I was determined to do it. I kept getting really bad headaches and feeling tired all the time, and there were times when I would burst into tears for no reason. But within a couple of weeks I had stopped taking it. I also cut down on the drink, and I soon put on a bit of weight and got a bit of colour back to my face.

I'd love to say that I felt rejuvenated being off the drugs but I think my body was so toxic it would have taken it months to get back to normal, but I definitely felt the best I had done in months.

I really thought this was going to be a new start for me and I was excited for the future. Edward has lots of connections in the modelling world so he offered to try and get me some work. He looked after me one hundred percent and would come on castings with me to make sure that the work wasn't sleazy. He didn't like me doing anything that involved me taking my clothes off. On one casting he argued with the casting director when he started scrutinizing me. I've had comments from casting directors about everything going before, and this one started saying similar things: that my teeth were too big and my nose was a bit of a funny shape. Edward jumped in and said, 'Oh for God's sake, she's not exactly a bad looking woman is she?' I've never seen anyone look so shocked. I don't think the all-important casting directors are used to having people standing up to them.

I got a couple of good catwalk shows through Edward and he also put me forward for a campaign for Pretty Polly, but unfortunately I didn't get it because I couldn't position my legs in the right way! He also got me a job modelling for Graduate Fashion Week, which is the one below London

Fashion Week, at a venue in Battersea, South London. A lot of big models were doing it and when I walked into the toilet there was a girl sitting on a toilet seat with the door open injecting heroin between her toes. It wasn't the first time I'd seen someone do it and I knew it wouldn't be the last, but she was so pretty and I remember thinking what a waste it was that she was doing that to herself. It's funny how I couldn't see that I was doing the same to myself.

Drugs are so easy to get at fashion shows. There were always lots of big businessmen around who would give the younger girls drugs. It was like an open secret. I once walked into a backstage room at a fashion show and saw a girl who couldn't have been more than 15 having sex with a businessman who looked about 40. She should have had her mum with her and her agent obviously wasn't keeping an eye on her. I do think there should be a legal limit on the age of the girls who are used in these shows because they're so vulnerable.

I think Edward has got a bit of a habit of finding waifs and strays and putting them back on the right path. He looked out for me like nobody else ever had and we had so much fun together. He used to ring me all the time and he made me feel safe and wanted. Unfortunately at the end of February things started to fizzle out between us. We stayed in touch but I always got the feeling that he felt like he'd put me back on the right path and now he wanted me to stand on my own two feet. Sadly I still wasn't strong enough to do that.

Chapter 13

SPECIAL K

Come March 2006, even though Edward had introduced me to lots of new people, the modelling work was drying up once again, mainly because I still couldn't be bothered to go along to any castings. But I couldn't stop my partying. I hadn't heard from Edward so I assumed my New Year's escapades had put him off me, so I threw myself back into clubbing and my desire for coke came back with a vengeance. Taking coke was something I didn't even think twice about, and if I ever found myself without some there was always someone who would share theirs with me.

I've lost count of the amount of times I've found myself in toilet cubicles with complete strangers and a rolled up note in my hand, hovering over lines of white powder. If I was planning a night out I wouldn't even consider going without either having coke on me, or knowing where I could get some. I don't know what I thought I was going to do when my money ran out. I didn't worry about it.

I started going out to clubs all the time, sometimes five times a week. I'd get back home, sometimes at seven in the morning, sleep all day, and then get up and do it all over again. The main places I went were Paper, Chinawhite, Kabaret, Movida, Funky Buddha and Isis. There was a group of us who moved around together night after night. I'd like to say we were a group of friends, but we were just the good time kids. We were coke buddies who would have run at the first sign of any one us being in trouble. It was a very unreal environment.

Quite a lot of celebrities used to hang out on the club scene. One person I always used to see was Paul Danan, who used to be in Hollyoaks. He bought me a bottle of champagne on my birthday once. I don't remember it happening but I read about it in the paper a few days later so it must have happened! Sarah Harding was always out as well, but I never spoke to her. She always looked a bit sad and lost, but always absolutely stunning.

I met loads of people through the club scene and I probably became one of the West End's most pro-lific clubbers, so I was always getting invited to par-ties that went on after the clubs closed. I often used to go with a friend of mine called Sarah who I had randomly met in Movida one night. Well, I say friend but we were only ever really partying partners and she certainly wasn't the kind of person I would have been able to turn to if I had a problem.

One night while we were at Chinawhite we were invited to a party at a flat in Putney. The guy who owned the flat, Eduardo, worked in TV and he was really flashy. The flat was amazing and had this huge roof terrace that looked out all over London. Everywhere you looked there were dugs, including Ketamine, which is a horse tranquiliser. There was one girl wandering around in her underwear absolutely off her head on Ketamine. She'd done a line of it because they told her it was coke and she obviously didn't have a clue what she was doing. No one seemed to care that she was walking into doors and she looked like a zombie. At one point she started screaming and freaking out because she didn't know what was happening to her. When you do Ketamine you almost go into a black hole where nothing else matters. You can't communicate with anyone else and if you get trapped in your own bad thoughts, it's almost impossible to lift yourself out of it until the drug wears off. You don't feel like you've got any control over what you do or what anyone else will do to you. It's absolutely terrifying. I only tried it once and I will never do it again. I think it's the closest to hell I've ever been.

There was another girl at the party who – and this is one of the grossest things I've ever seen – was openly injecting heroin between her legs. *Right* between her legs. Models often inject themselves in places where the marks can't be seen, such as between their toes and underneath their tongues, but I had never seen something like that happen before. I was absolutely disgusted, and I'm not someone who gets offended by things very easily.

Eduardo seemed to have a never-ending supply of coke and he wasn't shy about sharing it. Every time we finished a gram he'd produce another one and start chopping out lines. I have no idea how much I did that night but it was more than I'd ever done before. But instead of giving me the usual brilliant high I started getting really paranoid. I decided that there were too many people at the party and that they were out to get me. I started thinking that maybe I'd been lured there so that people could hurt me. Everyone was going up to the roof terrace to dance but I refused because I became convinced that someone was going to try and throw me over. A lot of the models who were there were taking a drug called GHB, which is often used as a date rape drug. If you use it in small amounts it makes you feel like you're drunk and it's got no calories in it, so all of these girls who were paranoid about putting on weight would add it to diet coke and drink it. If you drink too much of it you could kill yourself, but you'd have to drink a hell of a lot so I guess they thought they would take their chances.

In the end I bolted it out of there and got a taxi

home. I didn't even tell Sarah I was going, I literally ran down the stairs and out the main doors as if I was running away from some kind of monster. I had to go down about 15 flights of stairs because I was too scared to get into the lift. I thought that if I got in there I would be trapped forever.

A short while later I went to another party in a tower block in Clapham. This male model invited me and when I arrived loads of girls were in the kitchen doing Rohypnol. Even in my drunken, drugged up state I knew how stupid that was. One of my friends was bragging saying that she loved her drugs and she asked for some to be put in her drink, so I grabbed it off her and chucked it down the sink. Just like the last party, I felt really uncomfortable there. There were loads of really bitchy girls and I started to get paranoid again, so I decided to leave. As I passed this room on the way out the door was open and these were these two girls rolling around on the bed together naked while the model who had invited me was sat there watching them, naked from the waist down. It was all so incredibly seedy and no one seemed to have any inhibitions.

I went to another party in this massive house near Park Lane that was owned by an Arab. It must have been worth millions and it had cameras in every room so no matter where he was in the house he could see what was going on everywhere. Again, there was a never ending supply of drugs and people were spilling drinks on what looked like very expensive rugs and tables, but he didn't seem to care. I was at that party for two days in total. We all sat around this table doing countless grams of coke and talking rubbish. In the end we only left because someone opened up the curtains, turned the lights on and asked everyone to leave. I don't know how long I would have stayed there otherwise. I didn't ever want to leave. It was one of the nicer parties and while I was there it felt like the outside world didn't exist.

The kind of people I was hanging out with back then were horrendous. They all thought they were someone even though they weren't. They thought because they had money they had power and they could buy anything they wanted. And to be fair, they probably could. Drugs and women were readily available for the right price. A lot of them didn't work because their parents were rich so they were spoilt and did what the hell they wanted. I find it hard to believe that I thought it was all so glamorous. I truly believed that these people were my friends, that we were one big crazy gang who didn't give a shit about anything other than getting high.

Somehow, and I still find it hard to believe now, I managed to land myself a couple of modelling jobs around this time, but I was rapidly getting myself a bad reputation for being incredibly unreliable. I also didn't look great but I happily took any work

I could get.

I did one fashion show for a range of jewellery and I drank before, during and after the show, so by the time it finished I was decidedly wobbly. There was a huge after party at a club called Crystal that's just off Oxford Street and I was really excited about it. I went along with some of the other models and I was drinking loads and loads of champagne. I don't remember much about the evening but I know that I fell on a table and a bouncer escorted me out. I decided that I wasn't done with partying for the night and I wanted to go on to another club so I started walking in the direction of Chinawhite. I was so drunk I got completely lost and ended up somewhere down by Edgware Road, which is totally the wrong direction. I spotted a courier van parked up so I opened up the passenger side door, got in and told the driver to take me to Chinawhite. Amazingly, he did. I was such an idiot getting into a car with a complete stranger but I had no concept of fear when I was that wrecked.

My plan was to go into Chinawhite and find some of my friends, but as soon as I walked up to the door this guy I know called John Stephen, who is one of the managers, told me in the nicest possible way that I was way too drunk to go in.

He whistled for a black cab and told the driver take me home. I was so drunk I'd lost my phone and my purse, so he lent me money for the cab and also gave me his spare mobile so I could contact someone in case I got into any kind of trouble. But I made the taxi take a detour to another club called Hedges and Butler where I knew there was another party going on. Thankfully they let me in and it was an amazing do. I did a few lines to sober up and I was ready to have a good time, but as soon as I sobered up I realised that it was all very civilized in there. Lily Cole was there and she looked stunning; so healthy and serene. I was also talking to a girl I was convinced was Lizzie Jagger for ages, but when I mentioned her dad Mick she looked at me blankly. I had got the wrong person. God knows what all the people in there thought of me. It was a really small place and I didn't know anyone so I was wandering around chatting animatedly to anyone who would talk to me. I don't have a clue how I got home that night but I guess I must have got a taxi with the money John gave me. I did pay it back to him and also returned his phone. God knows where I would have ended up if he hadn't helped me out.

The following week I got booked for a fashion show for an up and coming French designer. It was quite a big deal and it would have been a good chance for me to show the modelling agency that I was okay and hopefully get some more work off the back of it, but I totally, utterly f'd it up. I decided that it would be really funny to do an E and drink half a bottle of vodka before the show to make it a bit more fun. The thought of walking up and down the catwalk for ages filled me with dread so I thought the booze and E would make it less of a chore. I didn't really like E's and had only done them a few times before, but they were a lot cheaper than coke and it was all I had on me at the time so I thought 'why not?'

The main part of the show went okay. Then as a finale all the models had to walk in a line down the catwalk. I was really coming up on the E and there was really loud music pumping out, so I stepped out of the line and did a little dance on the stage. I thought it was hilarious. One of the women involved in the show stormed up to me afterwards and gave me a huge telling off, but I just laughed in her face. She was quite rightly furious and called my modelling agency to complain and I was put on a warning. Any more bad behaviour and I was out.

I knew I had to behave or they agency were going to drop me, so when I got booked for a show for a big underwear company I absolutely had to behave myself. Some of the EastEnders cast were there, as well as a few other celebs who were all sitting at the side of the catwalk. As I walked down the catwalk past James Alexandrou, who plays Martin Fowler, he shouted, 'Toss me off' in my direction. I was so shocked that I laughed. I wasn't expecting to hear that. I got really told off by the woman running the show for laughing, but I couldn't really tell her what he'd said. Thankfully she didn't report it back to the agency. It would have been annoying if I'd got sacked over something that wasn't actually my fault. OK! magazine was covering the event and it was all quite showbiz. Joe Swash was there and I had a good chat with him and he was lovely. It was one of the few shows that I actually enjoyed.

After the show I was sitting at the bar and these two really posh guys asked me of I wanted to go on to another party with them. The bar was thinning out and I was quite drunk so I didn't need to be asked twice. I jumped into their convertible with them and off we went. It was so stupid because they could have been anyone, but I didn't care. They took me to another bar where we drank loads of champagne. I started to feel really drunk so I decided to do a line of coke to sober myself up a bit. I didn't tell them what I was doing in case they didn't approve, but I needed something to help me to think straight as I was all over the place.

The guys offered to drive me home and even though alarm bells started ringing because they were as drunk as me, I put all my worries to the back of my mind and got back in the car. It was only when I was sat there that I realised just how dangerous the situation was. We were in Knightsbridge at the time and I suddenly remembered that Edward lived in Gloucester Road, so as we passed it I made them drive me to his house. I was praying he'd be in because I was starting to feel really uncomfortable. I banged on the door for ages and told the guys they could go and that I'd be fine to wait on my own. I had to weigh up whether I'd be safer standing on the street in the dark on my own or getting back into a car with two total strangers who could do anything to me.

I was so relieved when Edward eventually came to the door. It was about two in the morning and he'd been fast asleep so I threw my arms around him, said thank you and then dived into his house. One of the guys from the car tried to follow me in and Edward had to virtually shove him out the door and close it on him. Thank God he was there to come to my rescue.

Of course now I look back and think, 'What was I thinking getting into a car with two strangers who were drunk?' But back then I didn't care about that kind of thing. I didn't consider consequences of anything I did.

Chapter 14

PARTY ANIMAL

I was back doing around three grams of coke a day by now. The Gavin Henson story money had long since run out but I was making some money from doing the odd interview here and there for magazines, and also from the modelling. Because I was buying quite a lot of coke at one time I had three different dealers on hand so I knew I could always get hold of it. One of the dealers used to carry his coke around disguised as a bar of Dairy Milk. It was this huge block that was wrapped in silver paper and it even had the wrapper on. One time when he came to drop some drugs off to me he left it on my kitchen sideboard while he went to the toilet, so I snapped a bit off. It was at least ten grams, which is worth about £500, but I was desperate. I knew that would keep me going for a while. I quickly hid it in one of the cupboards and my heart was pounding when he walked back into the room, but he didn't even notice. It was such a stupid thing to do and God knows what he would have done if he'd realised. You really don't mess with those kinds of people.

I went with him to collect his big delivery of drugs once because he had run out and I was desperate for some. We drove to a car park in Chiswick, a guy came up and put the drugs though the window, he paid the money and we drove off. It made me laugh that the dealer must have made fortunes but he still had to use a really old Nokia phone all the time. It had no GPRS so it couldn't be traced, meaning that the police didn't know his whereabouts if they tried to track him.

I started doing a gram of coke each morning. As soon as I woke up I would reach for my drugs and sit in bed until I felt myself leveling out. My depression was at an all-time high and it was the only thing that helped me. I was still taking Xenical and loads of Valium to help me sleep each night, and I also started taking the anti-depressant Xanax again. Nothing really seemed to have much of an effect on me though. I think I was in such a dark place that the thing that was destroying me was also the only thing that could make me feel better.

I would be walking down the street and I'd realise that I need a quick hit so I'd dip my key into my little bag of coke and snort it there and then. How I never got caught out I don't know. I nearly got busted once when I went to London Bridge tube station and there were loads of police there with sniffer dogs. I had to turn on my heel and jump in a cab home because I had about five grams on me.

I also got thrown out of a gay club once for doing drugs. My friend Peter got caught doing a line in the toilet so the bouncers searched me as well. Peter was wasted and started shouting, 'You can't do this to me, I know the owner!' which was a total lie. The bouncers marched us to the door and I turned round and said, 'Look, I don't mind being thrown out, but can I please have my drugs back?' Surprise, surprise, I didn't get them. It made me laugh though because it was a gay club and you could buy drugs over the bar if you knew the right people. Talk about double standards!

Peter and I decided to cut our losses and go to Chinawhite instead. While we were there I got invited to another one of the notorious after parties. A very famous model I had met a few times before was going and she asked me if I fancied it. She was really well known so I thought it was bound to be a glamorous event if she was going. In fact, it turned out to be anything but.

As with all the other parties there were loads of drugs around and this particular model was doing some of the biggest lines I've ever seen. She didn't seem to care who saw her even though it would have totally ruined her career if it had got out. I had heard stories about how she was going off the rails but then she did something that shocked even me. We were sitting on the sofa with another model and she turned to her and asked if she wanted to make a porn video with her. She said that she'd been offered £250,000 to do one and that she'd split the money with her. She explained, while laughing loudly, that all of her money had been spent on drugs and partying and that she desperately needed the cash. I assumed that she would have hundreds of thousands in the bank, but she said she needed to get hold of money quickly as all of her savings had gone. As far as I know she never did make the video, but it was sad to think that she'd gone from being a household name to trying to sell herself like that.

The other girl turned down her offer, but that didn't stop them spending most of the evening snogging. As soon as people got stuck into the drugs at those kinds of parties anything went. It was always very drug hazed and sexual, but people viewed it as normal behaviour. A lot of people swung both ways. Well, if they didn't before they got to the parties and got trashed, they did once they got there. Hence there were always a lot of orgies going on. People would just roll up and join in. I only ever kissed one girl at one of the parties, after a massive coke binge. It didn't seem like a big deal and I didn't regret it the next day. It seemed kind of bohemian and what everyone else was doing.

Sometimes, however, things did go way over the top at those parties. There was a famous playboy at the same party as the famous model, who is known for being a terrible ladies man. He was there with his girlfriend of the time, who is also a household name. I walked into the kitchen to get a drink and when I went back into the living room I was stunned to see the playboy having sex with his girlfriend while she snorted lines off of the table, in full view of everyone. She had her back to him so she couldn't see what was going on, but there was another man filming the whole thing. She was so out of it that she had no idea she was being videoed, but I heard later that she found out about it and was completely paranoid that it was going to get leaked onto the Internet. She dumped the playboy immediately and still to this day they don't speak.

I was probably doing one modelling job every couple of weeks by this point. Then I started getting offers from one of the modelling agencies I was signed with to do escort work. They kept saying that I wouldn't be expected to actually *do* anything with the clients, but it all sounded very suspect and no matter how bad things got I told myself that I would never sleep with someone for money.

I got an email one day from the agency with the offer of a trip to the South of France on a yacht. It was to hang out with a member of foreign royalty and when I scrolled down and saw the email conversation that had been going on between the clients' representatives and the agency it was very clear to me what was expected of us. Even though we were assured that all we'd have to do was go along and chat to the client and his friends and be polite and fun, it quite clearly stated that all the girls were expected to go topless.

They call that kind of work 'commercial modelling', but there isn't actually any modelling involved whatsoever. It made me angry that the agency even suggested that I do it. They knew I was messed up so they probably thought I was easy prey.

I was also offered work 'escorting' celebrities for £500 a time, although I would be expected to go to their houses rather than out for a meal or anything. What kind of a person wants someone to go around to their house to keep them company but doesn't expect anything more? Again, even though I was desperate for money I refused to do it.

It had got to the point where one of the two agencies I was still signed with knew what a state I was in, so they thought they could get away with sending me to do any job and I'd do it because I'd be glad of the work. I don't know how they can even call themselves modelling agencies. A lot them are just glorified pimps. But then I got a call that made me feel excited for the first time in ages.

I had signed up with yet another agency in the hope that they would actually get me some decent work, and the boss of the company called me and said that he had some TV presenting opportunities coming up which he thought I would be perfect for. Presenting wasn't something I'd ever really thought about doing but I've got a really outgoing personality so I thought 'Why not?' I didn't have anything to lose and it would probably be good pay.

I was surprised they even considered me though because I was looking the worst I had ever looked. My legs were like twigs because I looked pale and exhausted, but I told myself that it wasn't anything a bit – or rather *a lot* – of make up wouldn't fix.

I was given the addresses of two TV companies so I put on my smartest clothes and headed down to the first one. I was asked to sit down in front of a camera and chat away about whatever I wanted. The guy in charge was all smiles and told me he really liked my presenting style. Then he asked me if I could do it again with my top off. I flatly refused. He explained to me that the job was for a 'specialist' men's channel so I would be expected to wear revealing clothes, or none at all. I was so upset. I didn't even bother to keep the appointment with the other TV company. I knew that they would expect me to do the same thing and I hadn't stooped so low that I was going to end up doing soft porn on a digital TV channel.

I hit a real low that day and I called my friend Holly and asked her if she wanted to go out partying. I hadn't seen her since our trip to Paris several months earlier, but she was as into clubbing as me and we always had a good time together.

We got all dressed up and went up to town and within an hour of being in Aura I had done three massive lines of coke and downed four double vodkas. Holly and I had a totally mad night which came to an abrupt end when I had a row with the man I saw filming the playboy and his girlfriend at that party the month before. I was so disgusted at what he'd done I called him every name under the sun and chucked my drink over him, and was promptly ejected from the club. I think I'm probably still banned now.

I was drink driving a lot at that time so I could save money on taxis, which are notoriously expensive in London. I would drive into central London and park my car near whatever club I was going to, then get wasted and get in my car and drive home. Coke helped me to concentrate and sobered me up a bit so I always used to do a line just before I left to make sure I could concentrate.

One evening I was in Chinawhite and I was absolutely legless. Fraser was there and we had become good mates and he was going to come back to my house so we could carry on taking drugs. I was there swinging my keys around on my finger and a friend of Fraser's told him that there was no way he could let me drive, but he didn't care. Another friend of mine called Naomi was supposed to come back with us as well but she refused to get into the car with me and stormed off to get a cab.

I left the club at about 3.30 and I don't really remember getting into my car, but I do remember pulling up alongside this group of guys at some traffic lights. For some reason I wound down my window and said to them in an Australian accent, 'Excuse me mate, do you know where any of the clubs are around here?' They were like, 'This is the West End, they're everywhere!' I laughed my head off and zoomed off.

We got to Knightsbridge and I was going quite fast and without even realising it I went straight through a red light. When what I'd done hit me I started screaming so I pulled over. I thought I was going to be sick; I could easily have caused a crash. All I wanted to do was go home and have another line and calm down. I was still shaking when I got home but half a bottle of vodka made me feel a whole lot better and by morning I'd forgotten that it had even happened.

I didn't let that one bad drink driving experience put me off and the following week I found myself drunkenly trying to get my key into the lock of my car outside Funky Buddha. Fraser was with me again and this time I was even more wasted and I got paranoid that I was going to crash. I was literally going about ten miles an hour watching the road in front of me. Other cars kept beeping me and over-taking but I totally ignored them. I was hunched over the steering wheel with my nose practically pressed against the windscreen just so I could see where I was going and I must have looked com-pletely ridiculous.

I wasn't even out of central London when I saw these blue flashing lights in my rear view mirror. The police pulled me over and they walked over and opened my car door. I'd been leaning on it and because I was so drunk I fell straight onto the floor. They breathalysed me – not that they needed to do that to tell I was drunk, I couldn't even stand up – and they told me that I was three times over the limit. They started shouting at Fraser for letting me drive in that state and then they put me in the back of their car and took me to a police station in West London. I was locked in a cell overnight while I sobered up. They took my shoelaces away from me in case I thought about hanging myself and they left me sitting there swaying from side to side. Thankfully I had done all my drugs so I had nothing on me. Fraser was the one with all the drugs but they didn't bother searching him.

It was freezing cold in the cell so I didn't sleep, and once I started to sober up I got edgy and pan-icky. I kicked up a bit of a fuss but this police officer told me that the more of a fuss I made, the longer I would be kept there. I didn't sleep a wink and they didn't let me go until eleven o'clock the following morning. I felt like hell by the time I got home. I was shivering and pacing the room, so I took couple of Valium and went to sleep. A few months later I had to go to court where I pleaded guilty to drink driving. I got banned from driving for three years. I know it was totally my fault but I never forgave Fraser for not stopping me driving and I didn't ever speak to him again. He knew I was in no fit state to drive and he was supposed to be someone who cared for me so he should have done something to stop me.

In a way I guess I was lucky I got caught because I would have carried on drink driving and could easily have hurt someone else or myself. Of course I didn't see that at the time. I thought the only good thing about getting banned from driving was that I had an excuse to sell my car. It was one of the only things I had in the world that was worth anything. I had already sold and pawned loads of stuff to get cash over the past year. The only things I never parted with were a ring of my Grandma's, which I still wear to this day, and a Rolex watch that my dad bought me for my 18th birthday. In fact, the box the watch came in was where I used to keep my drugs safe. It was like my special drug place.

I advertised my car on Gumtree and I got £850

for it; much less than it was actually worth. I went straight out and bought some coke with the money and reasoned that at least the money I would save on tax, insurance and petrol could now be spent on taxis.

I started hanging out with Holly a lot more and I'd often go over to her flat in Maida Vale where we'd sit up all night doing drugs and talking.

I knew another dealer in that area that we used to use a lot. Holly and I arranged to meet him one night just around the corner from her place to get some coke. We got into his car and I sat in the front to do the deal while Holly got in the back. She looked down and saw that he had some of the drugs were stashed under his seat. They were poking out and there was bag upon bag of white powder, so she couldn't resist stealing some. I ended up doing six grams that night and we were both really pleased with ourselves because we'd only paid for a fraction of that.

After that night we started to steal drugs from the dealer regularly. It was always the same routine. I knew that he fancied me so I would sit in the front and distract him while Holly sat in the back and stole some of this stash. She never took so much that he would notice and we did it for a good couple of months before he caught us. We claimed it was the first time we'd ever done it and that we were desperate. He started to get angry and threaten us, but we both laughed and said, 'What are you going to do? Call the police?' We should have been worried about what he'd do but instead we thought it was funny. He could have had a gun or anything, but we were like two naughty schoolgirls.

One night I went over to Holly's and we planned to have a big session. We bought three grams each and a couple of guys that she knew came over with two more grams and some champagne. I don't think my nose left the CD case all night. The boys didn't seem to be doing much of it so Holly and I must have done most of it between us. I would estimate we did about four grams each, and it was a lot stronger than anything I had done before.

All of a sudden my head started spinning and I started hallucinating. The room was really smoky and Holly and one of the guys, Sam, went into the kitchen. The other guy, Len, started talking to me about how his sister had been in rehab and for some reason he made me feel really nervous. I started to get really freaked out about every little thing. I heard Luke saying something to Holly about a 'middle man' and I suddenly started screaming, 'You're the middle man! I know you're going to hurt me!' The next thing I knew I was out of the door and running down the street. It was about four in the morning and Holly ran after me but I was too fast for her. She was ringing and ringing me on my mobile but I wouldn't answer because I was convinced that they were out to get me. I didn't stop running until I got to near Paddington and then a guy in a car pulled over and asked me if I was a prostitute which scared me even more.

I flagged down a random car and asked the man driving to drop me at The Hilton Hotel in Paddington. He could have been anyone but I was so off my head I don't even remember what he looked like. I remember that he also asked me if I was a prostitute, so God knows what I must have looked like. Thankfully he was a decent guy and he drove me to the Hilton and made sure I was in the door safely before he drove off again. As with all the other times, I could so easily have picked the wrong car to get into and ended up in all kind of danger.

I had no money so when I got to The Hilton I called Peter in hysterics. He told me to get into a cab to his house and said he'd pay when I got there. The sun was coming up when I arrived and the light was really blinding in my eyes, like someone was shining a torch in them. Peter calmed me down a lot but I was still hallucinating so I pulled all the curtains in the house and then made Peter put sheets over them so that no light could get through. I was convinced that if people couldn't see me they couldn't get to me. I was completely and utterly paranoid. It was one of the worst experiences of my life and I wondered if I would ever come down.

I don't know if the coke had been cut with something dodgy, if it was very pure or if I just did too much, but I had never had a reaction to drugs that bad before. Thankfully I always carried some Valium on me so I took a couple and passed out. When I woke up the following morning I felt so, so stupid. It felt like it had all been a dream, it was so surreal. I wanted to know why it had happened and I started to worry about it happening again. I felt like I had gone temporarily insane it wasn't something I ever wanted to experience again.

That night was so terrifying that it put me off doing drugs. For three days. But let's face it, at that time it was something of a record. When I did do my next line I was very cautious about it, but as soon as it kicked in I was hungry for more and the horror of that night paled into insignificance. I reasoned that it was just a one-off and the chances of it happening again were very slim.

Chapter 15

HOW LOW CAN YOU GO?

After getting done for drink driving I decided to stop going out partying in the West End as much as I had been. Everyone knew I had been busted for drink driving and I felt quite embarrassed about it. I also couldn't afford to get cabs back from central London every night and I hated the night buses, so I decided that it would be easier and cheaper to go out locally. I still knew a lot of people from when I used to work in the pubs and a lot of them had started going to this new bar called Bar Below. It was just like a bog standard wine bar but it got popular really quickly. I guess everyone likes a new place to hang out and it become the place to go. I knew that anytime I went in there, day or night, there would be someone I knew in there.

One day I went along on my own and I met a girl called Fran. We were both on our own drinking at the bar and we started talking and we spent the rest of the evening chatting. She was about 37 and a teacher, and she seemed really smart. We soon became drinking buddies and we'd meet up a few times a week to gossip, drink and do coke.

A lot of people in Bar Below did drugs and it was like an open secret that the toilets were always being used by people who wanted a few lines. Fran and I used to share a gram or two every time we met up. One of my old dealers had started hanging out there so it was never a problem getting our hands on it whenever we wanted to. Which was most of the time.

One time Fran and I were having a drinking session and I went to buy some cigarettes from the machine. This old guy approached me and stood there smiling and watching my every move. He looked like he was in his late 60s. He had really wrinkly skin and really small eyes that had huge bags underneath them. He said to me, 'Excuse me, this is the VIP area.' He thought he was being really funny so I replied, 'If you think this is the VIP area you've been going to the wrong parties.' Then turned on my heel and walked away. When I sat down Fran said to me, 'Was that bloke just trying to talk to you? He's called Tony and he's a dirty old man. Stay away from him.' He sat and stared at me from the other side of the bar for the rest of the night. Something about him was very weird.

At chucking out time Fran and I went on to a late

night bar just around the corner. When we walked in this guy I recognised as being an England rugby player, and who was obviously drunk, stood up and shouted, 'Can I buy anyone a drink?' I'd never met him before in my life but I piped up, 'Yes please, I'll have a double vodka and lemonade when you're ready, and Wales to win the rugby world cup!' I think he was impressed that I knew who he was and when he bought my drink over to me he sat down and hooked his legs around mine under the table and started flirting outrageously.

We chatted all night and then Fran, the rugby player, his cousin and I all decided to head back to my flat for a few more drinks. We called a dealer called Jockey John and he came to drop some coke off. I'd known John for a long time and he knew all about me, and he thought it would be really funny to tell the rugby player about what happened between Gavin Henson and I. He told him everything from the fact that we dated to the all-important detail that I had gone on to sell a story about him. I was absolutely furious so I chucked John out.

I managed to get myself out of what could have been a very difficult situation by saying that the paper was going to run the story anyway, and all I'd done was given them a couple of quotes. The rugby player didn't seem to care about it anyway. In fact, if anything he seemed quite excited by it.

After another hour of full-on flirting he walked into my bedroom and beckoned me over. We started kissing and messing around and then all of a sudden he called Fran in and asked her to join in! How very romantic. Thankfully she declined his offer but needless to say it put me off him and I left him and went back into the living room with Fran to do some more coke.

He kept shouting at me to go back into the bedroom but I wasn't having any of it. Okay, so it wasn't like I was his girlfriend or anything, but I still didn't expect someone I'd just met to try and coerce me into a threesome. He ended up leaving at about six in the morning and tried it on with me again as he left, but I gave him a kiss on the cheek and laughingly said that was all he was getting.

I'd actually thought he was really funny and a nice guy up to that point, and it was only the next day when I Googled him that I found out he was married with a child. He must have taken his wedding ring off that night because he certainly wasn't wearing one and he definitely wasn't acting like a married man. I wasn't surprised when I didn't hear from him again. It made me sad to think that he'd obviously set out to pull someone that night, hence his lack of wedding ring, and probably hadn't given his family a second thought.

Having had a really quiet period work wise I got booked for a catwalk show the following week, but a few days before I went down with really bad tonsillitis. I was so skint I had to ask Fran to pay for my antibiotics, and even though all I wanted to do was curl up in my bed and sleep I got myself together and went to the job. It was paying a few hundred quid so I had no choice. I think because I was so toxic from the drink and the drugs the tablets reacted really badly with me and I started sweating terribly. I don't know how I made it down the catwalk but I was in a total mess. Again, it got back to my agency and they phoned and accused me of doing drugs. Ironic, really, as that was the one time I wasn't. Thankfully they believed me after I sent them a letter from my doctor and they didn't drop me as I feared. I was still fearful about the modelling work drying up completely.

I managed to stay away from central London and all the clubs and built up what I thought was a nice group of friends locally. One night Fran and I were walking to this Irish bar in Putney when this white van pulled up beside us. This cheery guy wearing a cap poked his head out of the window and asked if we were going to the pub. I laughed and said, 'Alright John?' because I recognised him immediately as John Leslie. He was with a mate called Rodhri Williams who I later found out was a Sky Sports presenter, and they both seemed quite funny, so we invited them to join us.

We all headed for a drink together and John was

being quite flirty with me. He was very charismatic and came across as a genuinely nice guy. I was doing quite a lot of coke and I offered it to John, but he turned it down. His reputation was already in ruins and his TV career was over and I think he wanted to keep his head down and stay out of trouble.

Me, John and Rhodri decided to go back to John's house so we called a cab and all bundled in. Fran said she didn't want to come back as she had to be up early the next morning, but as I'd spent the whole evening with the guys I didn't think twice about carrying on partying with them. They were a good laugh.

As soon as we arrived at John's place I got a call from someone from the news desk at the News Of The World telling me to get out of the house. He said to me, 'Amy, all the papers know you're at John's and if you don't leave now your life will be ruined.' I was known to the papers because of the Gavin Henson story, and I'd also met a lot of journalists on the party scene. I think it was pretty well known by then that I had a drug addiction so this guy was trying to help me out. I was quite out of it already so I giggled down the phone and said that I was a big girl and I'd take care of myself.

To this day I still don't know who phoned the newspapers to tell them that I was with John but I swear on my life it wasn't me. I wasn't even capable of thinking about selling a story, I was way too high.

I can only guess it was either someone from the pub who saw us all leave together and put two and two together, or it was Fran, who wanted to make a few quid on the side.

As soon as I put down the phone to the News Of The World a wannabe hotshot journalist from The People called me and asked if I was at John Leslie's house. Before I could even answer he told me he was sending someone over to hang out with me. I didn't really grasp why they were sending someone over. To look after me? To try and get a story? I was out of my head so I put down the phone and had another line. John was doing coke as well by this point and I remember laughing at him and telling him that he more around his nose than up it. He had these white circles on the end of each nostril as if he had frostbite or something.

We were all sitting around watching TV, doing coke and drinking when someone rang on the door-bell. I hadn't given anyone's John's address, but clearly The People already had it. John got a bit paranoid about answering the door because of all the drugs we had, but I told John it was just a mate of mine who was coming to join in the fun. He looked through the window to check and when he saw a girl of about my age standing there he let her in. We were in such a drug-addled haze that no one, including me, thought anything of the fact that I didn't even know her name. She introduced herself to everyone as Emma and although I didn't realise it at the time she was carrying a bag with a video recorder hidden inside. She set it down on the lounge table and immediately started recording everything that was going on.

The whole evening became incredibly seedy very quickly and it's all a bit of a blur. John had a piano and I remember playing chopsticks and singing Goodbye Norma Jean at the top of my voice while he joined in. Rodhri had been upstairs for ages and he suddenly walked into the lounge wearing nothing but a t-shirt and socks. I found out later that he'd been watching porn in one of the bedrooms and he was clearly still quite excited. He chopped out some lines of coke and started handing them around to us, calling himself 'waiter Williams'. I was happily snorting whatever was given to me while drinking large vodkas.

John and I went and sat down the sofa and we started kissing and fooling around. Things started to get quite heated so we went upstairs to his bedroom. He had this big box of dressing up clothes for some reason, and I put on these stockings I found and I was dancing around in them laughing. I found it all hysterical and John was giggling his head off too.

I ended up sleeping with John, although I don't really remember an awful lot about it. I know that he was very respectful and kept checking that I was okay. At one point Rhodri came into the bedroom to join in, but I didn't feel very comfortable with both of them there so John asked him to leave. He walked out sheepishly and went back into one of the other bedrooms to watch more porn.

I have no idea how much coke I did that night but I know it was a hell of a lot. Emma was there the whole time and she seemed to be having just as much fun as the rest of us. She eventually left around six in the morning and gave me a kiss goodbye as if we were genuine friends, and said she'd call me.

At about seven I was eating a bacon sandwich that John had made me. All of a sudden I felt like I wanted to get out of John's place as quickly as I could. We'd run out of coke and I was starting to have a comedown and was feeling pretty crap. In the cold light of day the gravity of what had gone on that night started to hit me. There had been a tabloid journalist there the whole night and she had been taking pictures of John and I getting off with each other, and also hoovering up line after line of coke. She must also have captured a semi-naked Rhodri, who until that point had a very clean-cut image. The fallout was going to be incredibly messy.

There I was sitting having breakfast with someone that was about to have their life ruined all over again, and someone whose nice-man public image was about to be shattered. And it was all because I had got completely out of it and allowed myself to be taken advantage of by a tabloid who didn't give a shit about me. They just wanted the story and to use my humiliation as entertainment. They didn't care that I was in need of rehab, not another kiss and tell story. They took complete advantage of the fact that I was a drugged up mess.

When my phone rang I nearly jumped out of my skin. It was a woman from the features desk at The People asking if I was still at John's. When I said I was she told me to stay there for as long as possible because they wanted to send a pap photographer down there to try and get shots of John and I leaving the house together. It wasn't even as if she was asking me, she was instructing me, and it made me really angry.

John drove me home and then he went off to watch football. He was very sweet when we said goodbye and gave me a kiss and said he hoped I'd had a good night. He even thanked me for making it so much fun and said that he hoped we could see each other again. I suspected he would change his mind pretty swiftly once he heard from The People.

I sat on my sofa crying for hours. I was coming down from all the drugs and my head was pounding. I didn't know what I could do to make myself better. I took a couple of Valium and went to sleep, but when I woke up I still had this feeling of complete doom hanging over me. As much as I wanted to there was nothing I could do to make the story go away. The newspaper had a video and pictures of everything that had gone on and there was no way they weren't going to run it. In a week's time the story was going to be on the front page and everyone was going to know just how much my life had spiralled out of control.

I felt sick when I thought again about the effect it would have on everyone involved. I desperately wanted to phone John up and warn him about what was going to happen but what could I say? 'By the way John, that girl who came to your house last night was actually a tabloid journalist. She videoed you and I taking drugs and sleeping together and now you're going to get totally stitched up in the paper.' All I could do was wait for the story to come out and hope it didn't sound too horrific.

I spent the whole of the next week drinking and taking coke. I was barely out of the pub. I thought if I didn't think about The People's story it would make it go away. I remember crying to Fran about it one night and saying that my life had become such a mess. She calmly said that there was nothing I could do and to think about the money I was going to be paid, but that made me feel even worse.

I was in the pub the Saturday before the article was coming out and a journalist from The People's features desk called me up and read the entire story down the phone. They always have to run it by the person who is selling the story first to make sure all the facts are correct.

I was standing outside the pub at the time having a cigarette and when I walked back in to finish my drink I fainted from the shock of what I'd just heard. The piece was so much worse than I'd imagined it would be. It made John sound sleazy, which he wasn't. In fact, it made him sound like a total pervert. It described how he 'pushed me against the wall with his shovel-like hands' which was just ridiculous. He was actually very gentle and caring with me that night.

The day the article came out was one of the worst of my life. I got a furious text from John calling me a few choice names and saying how devastated he was. A piece then went in the Daily Sport a couple of days later with the headline 'Stripped teased and mad for it' which detailed everything that had gone on and managed to make it sound ever worse than The People story, which I didn't think was possible. John sent me another text telling me that his mum was in such a state about the tabloid revelations she was having a nervous breakdown over it all. I sat down and cried for about the tenth time that week. How could I cause someone that much pain? I hated myself.

My mum was also absolutely horrified when she saw both stories. She called me up to confront me and all I could say to her was, 'Mum, not everything you read in the papers is true you know.' More than anything I needed her to support me and tell me everything was going to be okay, but who can blame her for being so angry and disappointed in me. She was going to have to face her neighbours whispering when she walked out the door, and it was a cruel position to have put my family in. If only I had stopped and thought about it at some point. *Any* point.

Some of my old school friends also got back in touch via MySpace saying how shocked they were about the story. Great, so now everyone knew just how much of a success my glamorous move to London had been. There was one nice one in amongst the jibes though, from a guy called Chris Ware who runs a gym called Funky Pump, who I had known in my running days. He was really upset for me and his immediate reaction was concern – he didn't recognise the Amy he once knew in the tabloid stories. He offered to get me back on my feet and train me for free so that I had something to focus on, but it would have meant me moving back to Wales so I ungratefully declined his offer. Of course I wish now that I had, but it was the last thing I was thinking about. We're still really good friends, though, and I'm so grateful to him for trying to help me.

Someone even also showed the paper to my Nan, which was mean and spiteful. There was no way she would have found out about the story otherwise, she never read those kind of papers. The last thing I wanted was her upset so I was furious. Of course it was my fault that the story was in there to start with, but someone showed it to her just to be malicious. What kind of a person does that? The funny thing is that she never, ever mentioned it to me. Even when we were watching TV together a while ago and John Leslie came on screen she didn't say a word.

I never heard from Rodhri again but by a complete twist of fate my cousin Tom happened to be working with him at Sky Sports at the time the story came out. Tom was at work on the Monday after the story broke and Rodhri came wandering into the news room, held his hand in the air and joked, 'I hold my hands up, I did it and I got caught!' He was obviously trying to laugh it off and everyone went along with it. Tom even turned around and said, 'Ah well, good on you mate. As long as she was fit. It's just a shame you got caught.' Up until that point Tom hadn't read the story, he'd just heard the main details filtering down from other people, so when he did get round to reading it in full on the internet he was absolutely horrified to discover that his own cousin was the girl involved. I'm pretty sure he wouldn't have been quite as encouraging to Rhodri had he known.

The married rugby player that I had snogged a couple of weeks previously clearly panicked when he saw the John Leslie piece and he got his agent to call up The People and ask them if they were planning to run anything on 'his client' and me. It was a bit of a stupid thing to do. I hadn't told any of the papers about what had happened between us so he basically just landed the rugby player right in it and admitted his guilt.

Someone from The People phoned me straight away and told me about the phone call, and then said that they wanted to take me out for a nice lunch. How stupid did they think I was? They obviously wanted to see me so they could get the story out of me, but I wasn't interested. I didn't want to sell the story and still to this day I won't name the rugby player involved.

Even if I *had* wanted to sell the story, I don't actually think the editor of The People would have let me. I heard on the grapevine that he had warned his staff to leave me alone because I was in such a mess. I think he thought that getting the story from me would have been a step too far. I was clearly in need of some help and after the John Leslie story he instructed his staff to back off.

I hadn't seen Edward for a while but I really missed him and he was one of the few people I knew I could trust. I also knew that he had my best interests at heart. I got Fran to phone him up and ask him if I could go over and stay with him for a few days. I needed to get away from Putney and from the same people in the same pub and have some space. He told Fran to put me in a cab straight away so I packed up some clothes and left immediately. The People wasn't the kind of newspaper that Edward read so I knew he wouldn't have seen the article, which was such a relief. I didn't want to have to try and justify myself to him when there was no way I really could.

When I arrived Edward gave me a kiss and made me a cup of tea. Then he sat me down and said to me, 'I've seen the article.' I was completely taken aback. It was the last thing I expected. He smiled gently and said, 'I've read between the lines and I can see what's been going on. I think you have something of a problem with drugs.' I wanted to cry knowing that he had read all these awful things about me. He was the one person that I wanted to think good of me. I got really defensive and tried to explain it away saying it was the first time I'd done drugs for ages, but it was hopeless. He could see by looking at me that I was an addict.

Poor Edward said that he blamed himself in a way. He said that he wished he'd stuck with me and looked after me and kept me out of trouble. But that wasn't his job, it was mine. I was a grown adult and I had made a lot of very bad decisions.

We talked for ages and I eventually I was really honest with him, telling him the full extent of my drug taking. I also admitted that I had a drug problem when we were together and that the real reason I had collapsed on New Year was due to drink and drugs.

I started sobbing and saying how upset I was that I had hurt John Leslie. I still had his number so he suggested that he call him and try to explain why I did what I did. I knew that if anyone could try and make him understand, it was Edward. I was afraid that John would slam the phone down on him – and he was well within his rights to – but instead he listened as Edward explained that I had a serious drug problem and was incredibly sorry for any pain I had caused him. John then asked to speak to me. He asked if I was okay and that he was sorry that we'd both got mixed up in such an awful situation. He said that he hoped I wasn't in any pain and that we would both feel better one day. I was stunned. This was a man that I had, to all intents and purposes, landed in a whole heap of trouble and helped to ruin his reputation even further, and yet he was worried about *me*. In return I told him how sorry I was, especially for hurting his mum, and we agreed that we had both been victims in a way. I'll always keep in mind how kind he was to me that day. He really had no reason to be.

After the phone call Edward told me to get my things together because he wanted to take me somewhere. I naively thought that we were going to go off for a nice relaxing few days in the country or something, but the next thing I knew I was in the back of a black cab on the way to The Priory rehab clinic in Barnes.

I know that The Priory has got this image of being a celebrity haven and as much as I didn't want to go to rehab, I thought that at least it would be comfortable there. I was wrong. I thought it was going to be like a glamorous hotel with a few therapy sessions here and there, but it was like a hospital with white rooms and a clinical smell, and it had a really tough regime. Edward's parting words to me were, 'Bohan, this will do you good,' but I already knew that I wasn't going to stay there. Of course part of me wanted to get better, but another part of me knew how hard it would be to sort myself out and I didn't have the energy to try.

As Edward was paying for the rehab I did feel like I had an obligation to at least see if I could work through some things. The doctors did an assessment on me to decide if I was going to be an outpatient or an inpatient. They clearly thought I was a bad case because they told me I would have to stay as an inpatient for some time. I was sharing a room with one other person and I found it almost impossible to sleep. I was craving drugs and alcohol like I never had before and I spent any spare time I had curled up on my bed crying. The doctors kept assuring me that I would get better but I was so paranoid I thought they were all lying to me. I had these horrible visions of them locking me in my room for days on end while I detoxed. I didn't speak to anyone other than the doctors while I was there. I didn't want to know what anyone else was in for or how much their life had improved since they got clean, I just wanted out.

After two days of wandering around like a zombie and being unpleasant to any doctor who tried to help me, I checked myself out and went home. I literally threw my belongings in a bag, walked out the front gate and hailed a cab. It was just too hard to stay there. I obviously wasn't ready to get clean because even though I knew the drugs were destroying my life, the thought of letting go hurt me so much more. It was easier for me to go around in a daze for more of my life than actually have to face up to anything. And besides, I knew that my payment from The People would be waiting me for me at home and that meant one thing and one thing only: I could buy more drugs.

Chapter 16

CAREER
KILLER

I was clearly an easy target when I was at my lowest point and I was being used by people all over the place. I ended up getting paid about a quarter of what I should have done for the John Leslie story. After all the pain and upset I got a few grand, which was not even close to what I should have been given. If I hadn't been so dependant on coke I may have done the right thing and refused the money altogether, but I was so broke that wasn't even an option.

I suspect the paper knew I wasn't really capable of thinking properly so they gave me a really low amount knowing they could get away with it. They were just trying to make money from me in the same way that Jenny had with Gavin Henson. The funny thing is that apparently after the John Leslie story had been in the papers she phoned someone very high up at The People and had a massive go at them saying that they had effectively ruined my life by printing the piece. When I heard that I had a little bit of respect for her and thought that maybe she had turned over a new leaf. Then I got a call from her saying that if I ever had another story like that I should go through her because she could get me a better deal. Rather than being annoyed that The People had run the story because she was concerned about me, she was annoyed that she didn't get a cut of the fee. So much for caring about my welfare. She was just one of many people trying to make money out of me because I was vulnerable.

Nobody was looking out for me apart from Edward, and even he'd had enough of me. He was furious when he found out that I'd checked myself out of The Priory, and who can blame him when he'd paid so much money to try and help me? I wasn't ready for help at that point and it's a shame to think that if I had been, I could have saved myself from all the nastiness of the following six months.

I think Edward pretty much gave up on me after The Priory episode and it makes me incredibly sad to think that I pushed away the one person who was truly there for me.

You would have thought that the John Leslie experience and my brief time in rehab would have been a massive wake up call for me, but instead it sent me on a massive downward spiral. Some people treated me like I was complete dirt after the story came out, and I started to believe that I was. I had a serious case of self-loathing that was getting worse by the day. I felt so humiliated. All my friends from the party scene had totally dropped me because I hadn't been out in the West End for a while. Nobody bothered to get in touch and see how I was.

I can't say I was surprised when I pretty much stopped getting booked for modelling jobs altogether after the story appeared. I was only signed to one agency by this time because the others had given up on me because I was so unreliable, and also looking increasingly unhealthy. I did, however, somehow manage to book one job, which was to be my last for a very long time.

I was asked to do a catwalk show for a swimwear line in a club called Tantra. There was a gorgeous model there called Louise Glover who looked really curvy and healthy, while I felt like a scrawny mess. I kept comparing myself to her and thinking what could have been had I not gone down the drug route.

I had already done quite a lot of coke that day and I certainly wasn't trying to hide the fact that I was doing drugs. I could barely sit up straight, let alone stand up straight. I hadn't seen my friend Peter for a while but I called him up and invited him along to the show. We always had a laugh together and I needed something to cheer me up. We were on a mission to get wrecked. There were crates and crates of Moet and Chandon champagne and we drank a bottle each as soon as we got there.

I was called to the make up chair so they could get me ready for the catwalk, but the make-up artist took one look at me and stormed off to get someone else. She came marching back with this really camp guy who was wearing bright red braces. He looked at me, let out a little shriek and said, 'My God, *what* is *tha*t?' The make-up artist told him she couldn't do a thing with me because I had coke coming out of my pores and all the make-up was sliding off my face. You know like when you go for a run and you sweat? That's what I was like, only it was coke coming out of my skin not water. I'd just been for another line in the toilet and it was literally oozing out of me.

I was trying to sit up in the chair so I didn't look so bad, and Peter was trying to convince everyone that I looked okay. I remember him rather patheti-cally saying to this little crowd who had gathered around me, 'Oh come on, she doesn't look *that* bad. Just slap some more make-up on her and she'll be right as rain.' Only he was slurring, so he didn't really help my case very much. It was like something out of Absolutely Fabulous with all these gay men standing around looking at me in disgust.

I was told that there was no way they were letting me walk down a catwalk in that state, and then they asked me to leave. I just shrugged, picked up my bag and flounced off while all the other models looked on open-mouthed. Peter went off into Soho to party but I wasn't in the mood so I headed straight home to the pub to meet Fran. I laughed my head off when I told her about it. By that point I thought it was hysterical. It was only when I got a call from the agency saying that they no longer wanted to represent me that it didn't seem quite as funny anymore. That was it. My modelling career was well and truly dead, and I'd single-handedly killed it with my stupidity.

That was the last time I ever saw Peter because he moved back to Australia – where he's from – shortly afterwards. After all the fun we'd had together it seemed sad to end things on such a crappy day. We didn't even keep in touch. I guess we were never really proper friends. We only hung out together when we were on drugs so we may not even have liked each other had we not been high. It would have been nice to find out though.

I had no work at all and any agencies I tried to contact wouldn't even take my call or reply to my emails. I was living off the money I'd been paid for the John Leslie story but that wasn't going to last forever. But while I had it, I was going to enjoy it and then worry about paying the bills later. Something would come up, surely.

I had nothing better to do now than go to Bar Below every single day. I had money to pay for booze and no responsibilities so it seemed like the best option. I thought that the people in there genuinely liked me and it soon became like my second home. Fran was my partner in crime and every night after she finished work she would head down to meet me and we'd get drunk together and take coke in the toilets.

The wrinkly man that I'd first met a few weeks before was always in there staring at me. He often tried to talk to me but I would ignore him unless I was really hammered. He gave me the creeps. Then one evening towards the end of April 2006, when I was really drunk, he asked if I wanted a little pick me up. He pulled a small bag of coke out of his pocket and offered it to me, and even though I had my own drugs on me I took the bag from him and headed to the toilet. I would much rather do someone else's drugs that my own. It was a great way to save money.

By the end of the night I had finished all of my drugs and done half of his, so when he invited me back to his place to have some more drugs, I went. As far as I was concerned I was going to get the drugs and go back to mine on my own. I wasn't going to hang out with him or anything.

I told Fran I was going back to his house and she didn't seem at all bothered. The wrinkly man, who I found out was called Tony, told me that he was going to leave before me and that I should follow a few minutes later and meet him in a cab around the corner. I had no idea why he didn't want us to be seen leaving together, but I went along with it. As long as I got some free coke I didn't care.

Because I'd seen Tony in the pub so much and everyone knew him it didn't seem like a big deal going back to his place on my own, even though I didn't know anything about him. He did seem a bit odd but when we got to his place it looked lovely. He had a really flash Jaguar parked outside so I didn't think he could be *too* dodgy. It wasn't like he was taking me back to a dingy squat some-where.

The house was really nice inside. It was like this big three-storey town house and must have cost him a fortune. It was way too big for one person to live in on their own, and he must have sensed what I was thinking because he told me that his wife had recently divorced him because he got caught sleeping with his best friend's wife. He also told me he'd been in jail for smuggling calculators when he was younger. It was such a strange thing to say, but I just laughed along with him.

I sat on the sofa in his huge front room while I waited for him to get the coke for me. He asked me if I wanted a quick line before I left and he swiftly started chopping them out on this big hardback book that had a picture of Kate Moss on the front. He started telling me about how he ran an events company and he seemed to be quite a nice, friendly guy, and not nearly as creepy as I thought he was. I started to feel quite relaxed so I decided to stay for a while. We carried on doing a few more lines and when he went out to get us some drinks he left a big pile on the book, so I snorted some of it up gleefully. It was amazing to be given all these free drugs. I was always the same when I did coke – I wanted as much as I could get my hands on, and there seemed to be a never-ending supply that night. I would guess that I did around six grams in all, but I can't be sure because it just kept coming and coming.

Tony kept putting on Elton John's single Blue Eyes on the stereo, and whenever he left the room I would take it off and put some dance music on and start dancing around. He was plying me with champagne and I thought he was a bit sad, like a lonely old man who was giving a girl he didn't know coke and champagne just so she would hang out with him. He started topping my champagne up with vodka too. I'd never drunk that combination of alcohol before and coupled with the coke it knocked for me six.

At some point during the night I blacked out. I remember hearing Blue Eyes on repeat and then losing consciousness. When I came to there was still some coke on the table but Tony was nowhere to be seen. I was really confused about whose house I was in at first, and why I hadn't gone home. It was now light outside and when I looked at my watch I saw that it was ten in the morning.

I felt like something was wrong but I couldn't put my finger on it. I never wore matching socks because I could never be bothered to find a proper pair, and I remember looking down and thinking my socks were on the opposite feet to before. I shouted for Tony but he wasn't anywhere to be seen so I went outside and hailed a taxi and went home. I felt grubby from staying out all night and felt like I needed to have a long shower, so I showered, took a couple of Valium and went to bed.

I didn't get up until about four in the afternoon, but that was normal for me. A typical day for me would involve me getting up early to mid afternoon, having some vodka or wine and a line of coke to wake me up, and then heading up to the pub to drink for what was left of the day. Tony was always in the pub in the evening and from that night on he was always offering me drugs.

A couple of weeks later I ended up back at his house again. It was the same scenario with him plying me with alcohol and coke, and then me passing out on the sofa and waking up to find him gone. Again, I felt like there was something funny about what had gone on. I had built up a pretty good tolerance to alcohol and coke but I assumed that his coke must have been much purer than I was used to because it made me feel completely out of it. Usually coke makes me hyper and happy, but his seemed to chill me out and make me want to sleep.

I started going back to Tony's quite regularly and one morning after I left his house I was walking home at about eleven in the morning and I collapsed in the street. My legs just gave way underneath me and a passer by called an ambulance and stayed with me until it arrived. As soon as I arrived at hospital they gave me an ECG test to see if my heart was functioning okay and they also checked my blood sugar levels, which they said were really low.

They kept me in for a few hours before letting me go home. They told me to go home and rest and make sure I ate regularly. I think it was pretty clear that I'd been out on a bender. I decided that it was best to get back on the horse, as they say, so I went to Bar Below to have a couple of drinks. I stayed there all night, and at about midnight I got a text from one of the drug dealers that I used saying that he was going round to my house because I owed him money. I didn't have any money on me so I decided in my drunken stupor that it was best not to go home. I walked through the local park and then curled up on a bench and fell asleep. Thankfully it was early summer so it wasn't too cold, and I wasn't there long before these two policemen found me. One of them already knew who I was because he used to drink in Bar Below sometimes, so he put me in the back of the police car and drove me home. At least if the dealer has been waiting for me the police car would have scared him off.

The following week the same policeman had to drive me home again after I passed out while I was waiting for a night bus home. I had been too drunk to walk and too skint to get a taxi so the night bus seemed like the answer. I remember thinking the next day that after all that it was quite funny I got all the way home for free, even if it was in back of a squad car.

There were quite a few trips to Tony's house over the next month, and every time I went there I would wake up to find I'd blanked out certain parts of the night. I was out of it so much of the time back then that I barely knew what day it was. But despite that I still felt a bit uneasy about Tony. I liked his drugs, I just didn't like him and the way he acted around me. If we were in the pub he would almost make out like we were dating and I wondered what he was telling other people about us. Several times I got asked if there was anything going between us, and I could only think that he'd told his friends that we were together.

I told Fran how I felt about him but she assured me he was okay. She started coming along with me and she was just as happy to get the free drugs as

I was. Even though she knew I didn't like Tony very much, if he wasn't in the pub she would always ask me to text him and ask if we could go round because she wanted some coke. She was blatantly using me to get his drugs in the same way I was using him.

Fran soon found out where Tony kept his drugs – on top of his fridge – so she used to steal some whenever we went round, then we'd sneak off and share them back at one of our houses. It made me feel better when Fran was at Tony's with me because it meant I never got too out of it and passed out. She would always make sure I went home when she did.

Fran started calling Tony the Tambourine Man after the Bob Dylan song of the same name, because he would always make us follow him back to his place to get his drugs. He would play Blue Eyes and Perfect Day over and over again whenever we went round. It was odd because if Fran was there he would always make us ask him to chop out lines for us, but if I was there on my own he would just dish them out constantly and even let me do my own.

I sometimes got the feeling he didn't like Fran very much, but then he did ask us if we'd have a threesome with him one night so he must have liked something about her! Needless to say we both flatly refused. I found him physically repulsive and there was no way I would have gone near him in a sexual way.

As time went on I started to get increasingly freaked out by Tony. I was round his place with Fran one night when he locked her out of the house and took my phone off me. I was lying on the sofa out of my head and Fran was banging loudly on the door and demanding that he let her in. It was only when she threatened to phone the police that he opened the door. She immediately picked me up, put me in a cab and took me back to her place. None of us ever mentioned it again.

One Saturday afternoon a while later I was round at Tony's when a few people from Bar Below, including Fern, came to hang out and have some coke. When they got there they found me slumped on the sofa out cold. They panicked and thought I was going to die, but instead of calling an ambulance they put me in the boot of someone's car, drove to my house and dumped me in the front garden. I vaguely remember hearing people's voices but I was so high I didn't know what was going on. They obviously didn't want to call an ambulance to Tony's house because of all the drugs he had, so they decided the best thing to do was to get me out of there as quickly as possible.

They didn't even call an ambulance for me, they just drove off and carried on with their day, leaving me there. Thankfully the old lady who lived upstairs from me saw me and called an ambulance. I got taken to St Mary's Hospital and I was drifting in and out of consciousness. They gave me air and when I came to the doctor asked if I'd been doing any drugs. I said no but it was obvious I had been because it was all around my nose. The doctor was very off with me and I was only kept in for a couple of hours until I was more lucid, then they sent me home. There was nothing medically wrong with me, I had just come close to OD'ing and they clearly thought it was my own silly fault.

Tony started ringing me all the time and sending me stupid text messages, sometimes up to 15 a day. If I didn't reply he would call and text Fran saying I'd gone missing. She used to lie to him and say I'd gone into the West End, but instead we'd sit in her flat with the curtains drawn hoping he wouldn't come looking for me.

He also used to turn up at my house at all hours knocking on my front door, and I used to have to creep around so he wouldn't hear me. It was like he was obsessed with me. He wouldn't leave me alone. I told Fran that I wanted nothing more to do with him, drugs or no drugs. I think she was disappointed because that meant no more free coke for her, but she agreed to stop me going back to his place when I was drunk. Obviously I knew that if I went to Bar Below I would see him because he hung out there a lot, but I didn't want to be chased out of my favourite place by someone like him, so Fran and I carried on going there as much as ever.

One night Tony was looking for me everywhere and I was hiding at Fran's house as usual. She tried to throw him off the scent by saying that I'd gone to Chinawhite, even though I hadn't been for months. Incredibly he went up there looking for me. He paid around £20 to get into the club just to try and find me. It was all getting way over the top. Another time Fran told him that I had gone into rehab and that he should leave me alone, but he still kept calling me and leaving messages for me offering me drugs. He even called The Priory Clinic to see if I was staying there and kept insisting that they let him speak to me. I guess if I was off the drugs I was no use to him. He wouldn't have any power over me.

I avoided Tony as much as possible but I will freely admit that if I wanted drugs, sometimes I would call him and meet up, but only if Fran was there. I had got into a vicious circle where I had to have coke just to get my out of bed. If I didn't have any drugs I would stay in bed until the next day when I could get hold of some. If I didn't have them it would physically hurt. I had become so dependant on them that my whole body would ache if I went without them for a day or two. But sometimes I was so skint I had no choice but to see Tony. All the money I had been paid from the John Leslie story was spent on drink and drugs within about six weeks and I couldn't even pay my rent. I was constantly making up excuses about why it was late and I somehow managed to get away with not paying it for ages. So really, at that time Tony was my only option when it came to getting drugs and I will freely admit that I used him. Drugs were all I ever wanted from him.

I decided that I should try and get work somehow as I was desperate for cash, but I wasn't qualified to do anything and I wasn't capable of standing behind a bar for eight hours a day. I was too weak. I hadn't spoken to my friend Holly for ages but I decided that she may be able me out as she was very well connected, so I called her up.

Even though we'd been friends for a while I really didn't know much about Holly and she'd always told me she was a singer. However, during that conversation she admitted to me that she was a high-class escort. She was very beautiful and I could see how she would do well in that world. She suggested that I get into it as well because she was making a fortune. She said it was a good way to get money quickly, which was something I was desperately short of.

After giving it a lot of thought I signed up with an agency. I thought I could do it two or three times and get some money and maybe move away from Putney and make a fresh start somewhere, but when it came down to it I couldn't go through with it. The agency used to call me up while I was in the pub and tell me where I needed to be that night. I'd tell them I'd go, then I'd go back into the pub and sit there drinking all evening. When push came to shove, I couldn't have sex with someone for money, no matter how desperate I was.

the fact that I'd go back. Imagine Walk to own and promise to her Iad she ten Whole feed to see the hour not she had to see the own fire not she head to fire.

Chapter 17

THEY TRIED TO MAKE ME GO TO REHAB...

If I thought my drug problem in the early days was bad, it was nothing compared to how horribly addicted I had become. I was spiraling more out of control that ever and it got to the point where even Fran – who loved drugs almost as much as me – became concerned. I was barely eating so Fran used to call me up and make me go to her house so that she could feed me. I just couldn't be bothered to buy or make food. It wasn't my priority, drugs were. I wasn't washing either. I didn't have the energy. I would wear the same clothes day in and day out and I certainly couldn't afford to buy any new ones so most of what I owned was starting to look very tatty. I even slept in my clothes most nights because I would often pass out, then I'd get up the next afternoon and go out in them again.

One time when I went to Fran's house she ran me a bath and virtually forced me to get into it because

217

I smelt so bad. I never wore make up or washed or brushed my hair. I'd gone from someone who really looked after themselves and cared about their appearance to not caring one bit. I didn't mind that men wouldn't find me attractive or that people stared at me. I didn't care about anything.

I think it's safe to say I must have looked horrendous. One time I was walking to the pub smoking a rolled up cigarette and someone said to Fran that night, 'I saw Amy walking up the road today with a spliff in her hand. She looked like she was on heroin.' That was the final straw for Fran and she made an appointment at a nearby doctor's for me. I have no idea what I weighed at the time because I had pawned my scales months before, but anyone who looked at me could see that I was very thin and a total and utter mess.

I think at that point I was finally ready to be helped because I was scared for my life, but the doctor refused to put me into rehab. He told me that it was impossible for people to get addicted to coke and that I would have to go cold turkey on my own. Fran came into the doctor's with me and she started shouting at him saying, 'Look at the state of her. It's obvious she needs help, she could die!' But the doctor sent me away with a prescription for some super-strong painkillers that he said would help with the aching I would experience while I was coming off the coke. As if it was that easy! There was no way I was going to be able to give up drugs on my own.

I wasn't strong enough to try and get myself clean on my own so after just one day of abstaining I slipped straight back into my old pattern again. I was trying to avoid Tony so when some people I'd met partying at Chinawhite texted me and asked me if I wanted to go over and do some coke with them if seemed like a good option. I knew they weren't very nice people but they had drugs. I also knew that they didn't live far from me so I walked to their house as I didn't even have enough money for a bus.

When I arrived they had chopped out a couple of lines for me and I greedily snorted them up my nose. But afterwards I didn't get the usual hit I get with coke. I felt different. I asked what it was I'd been taking and someone laughed and told me it was crushed up E. They clearly didn't want to waste their expensive coke on me.

The whole vibe of the place was weird and even though I was high, something made me feel uneasy. I went into the kitchen to get a drink and that's when I saw all this camera equipment set up in there. Then I overheard someone in the other room say, 'We haven't got any red wine, what are we going to do?' Red wine is known for being the drink you hide date rape drugs in. Even in my messed up state something told me that I had to get out of there as quickly as possible, so I made my excuses and bolted out of the front door. It may have just been me being my usual paranoid self, but I got the feeling that bad things were going to happen in that house.

I hadn't eaten for days before I went to that house, and that combined with the E meant that I collapsed as I was walking home, this time on the main Putney Road. A passer by called an ambulance but this time they didn't bother to stay with me. They probably thought I was homeless or something, I looked so tatty. I was taken to hospital and given another ECG scan and then the doctor came to speak to me and asked if I'd been taking drugs. I said yes and laughed. I was still quite high so I somehow thought the fact that I'd ended up in hospital again was funny. The doctor was furious and gave me this big lecture before discharging me. I'm sure I should probably have stayed in there longer as I was in such a bad way, but I think he was so disgusted by my attitude that he didn't think I deserved help. I got in a cab and went home to bed and didn't get up for another two days.

When I told Fran what had happened she immediately took me to see another doctor who gave me Diazepam, which is like another form of Valium. I had to take two tablets three times a day to level out my mood, but they didn't have a big enough effect on me so I still felt like I needed the drugs. The doctor also promised to get me counselling, but it was taking forever to get an appointment though and I was feeling increasingly desperate. I was more paranoid than ever and even if I heard a door slam I would become convinced that it was someone breaking into my flat to try and kill me.

Fran went back to the doctor without me and explained to him the full extent of my problems. He promised her he'd try and get me into rehab and a week later I got sent an appointment for a local centre. Seriously, if I thought The Priory was bad, it was like a five-star hotel compared to the place he sent me to. I had to go for an initial assessment to this centre to see if they could help me, but when I arrived the place looked really run down and depressing. There were all these people sitting around it who looked like proper drug addicts. They were thin with sunken eyes and no expressions on their faces and it really freaked me out. I just looked at them and thought 'I'm not one of them, I shouldn't be here', and I turned around and went back home. One of the therapists at the centre called me and asked me to go back. They wanted me to do group therapy sessions with other people who were drug dependant, but I didn't want to be involved in anyone else's problems. I think a big part of someone's recovery is knowing that you're not alone and that you're not the only one with an addiction, but I wanted to concentrate on me and I thought it would bring me down hearing everyone else's sad stories. I said that I'd go along to the next session but when it came to it I couldn't bear the thought of it, so instead I stayed in bed and cried.

I did feel ready to do something to try and get better though, so I decided to go to a group near my home that wasn't quite as scary. It was an Alcoholics Anonymous meeting that someone told me about which was held in a church that was local to me. I thought that if I could at least stop drinking then maybe I wouldn't crave the drugs as badly.

I went along to the first meeting and I felt really positive about it. However, Fran told a few people in the pub that I had gone and when I went along for the second session I saw that Tony and a couple of the other guys from the pub had turned up too for a laugh. They thought it was really funny that I was going there. They told me they were going to come back the next week with even more people because it had been 'fun'. I felt so humiliated and I also felt really bad for all the people who were there that had genuine problems. They had made a mockery of it. After that I was too embarrassed to go again and I was so angry with Tony that I went round to his house and put a brick through the window of his Jaguar. I texted him and told him I was responsible and he didn't even bother to go to the police. He was probably too scared of what I would say to them if they interviewed me about it.

That whole AA episode really set me back and I continued on with my old life, dividing my time between my bed and the pub, befriending anyone who would buy me a drink or give me some coke. I was borrowing money all over the place and just about managing to stop my landlord from kicking me out.

A few people did try and help me here and there, but I would tell them they were overreacting and that I was getting better. It was always weird with Fran because as much as it seemed like she was trying to help me out, she would happily get me to call Tony if she wanted to get some coke. So I would end up having to see him, even though I hated him. But then, of course as soon as his coke came out again all was forgiven and suddenly his company didn't seem so bad. He never ever mentioned what I'd done to his car window and I never mentioned the AA meetings. It was as if it all had never happened. It was as if it was all one big game.

Tony still called and texted me constantly. If I ignored him he would come round to my house and post coke through my letterbox. It would be just enough for a line of two, so of course I'd do that and then be gagging for some more, so I'd call him up or go to the pub to find him. He knew exactly what he was doing. Not only was I hooked on coke, but he was the only person who would give it to me free so I was reliant on him in a way. I guess that made him feel needed and also gave him complete control over me. I didn't have a hope in hell of kicking drugs.

I'll never forget one of my lowest ever moments, which took place in Bar Below. Tony had given Fran and I his bag of coke so we could go and do some in the toilets, but when we got in there Fran dropped it on the floor because she was drunk and it went everywhere. It was a bit of a spit and sawdust type place so it wasn't always very clean. Needless to say the floor was all wet and covered in God knows what, but I was so desperate to get a hit that I bent down and started trying to snort the coke off of the floor, even though it had solidified. I must have looked absolutely pathetic and I cringe when I imagine myself scurrying around on the floor desperately trying to salvage some of the drugs.

In early July 2006 Tony invited Fran and I to a party at his house. Loads of people we knew were going so we thought it would be safe and quite fun. He introduced us to loads of local businessmen who all seemed really respectable, but they were freely doing coke off the garden table. Everyone started to leave, including Fran, so there was only me, Tony and another guy I didn't know left. I didn't feel comfortable so I went to go but Tony followed me and said, 'Don't leave Amy, look what I've got for you.' He pulled out what I thought was another wrap of cocaine, but then he told me that it was

crystal meth and that it was a present for me. I
chopped some out, but after just one line I went
absolutely crazy. Tony had this huge metal patio
table outside and somehow I got the strength to
pick it up and throw it across the garden. Then I
threw a chair at him and ran out of the front door.
I felt like I was completely and utterly out of control.
I literally did one small line and I felt like I'd done
three grams of coke in one go. My reaction even
scared me and it was the last time I ever tried it.

Chapter 18

CAMDEN CANER

I decided I had to try and get away from South West London and the scene I had become so involved with. I wanted to go somewhere new and so I started going to parties in Camden and Dalston, which had quite a hippy vibe. I had been told that I could get good drugs around Camden Lock, which as I later found out was a load of crap. The people there are so shady that if you ask for an E they'll spit it out into your hand. They keep their drugs in their mouths so that if the police come along they can swallow them so they won't get caught with anything on them.

I did meet a lot of nice people in the pubs and bars around there though, and I soon started to feel quite at home. I used to go to all the usual hangouts, like the Dublin Castle, Koko, Proud Galleries and The Hawley Arms. You could go to places on your own and make friends really easily. No one judges you there. There are always loads of celebrities around, like Sadie Frost, Peaches Geldof and Amy Winehouse, but no one even gives them a second glance.

I used to go to loads of parties there after hours but they were very different to the club parties I used to go to in a lot ways. Well, apart from the fact that they also lasted for days. Everyone would sit around strumming guitars and singing, and girls would walk around topless, thinking nothing of it. The parties were generally in empty houses or sometimes round at someone's flat, and it was like an open invite. Everyone was welcome.

People would come and go at all hours, and of course there were loads of drugs. Even if you were there on your own you weren't, if you know what I mean. Everyone was your friend. If someone had turned around and said, 'I may become a high-class escort girl to pay the bills,' people would go, 'Cool!' No one would even blink. Everything and everyone was accepted.

Camden became my bolthole for a while and I loved being able to escape there and be whatever I wanted to be. Of course I found people to get good drugs from so that was never a problem, and I went so often that generally I would walk into anywhere and know at least one person.

I was still hanging around in Putney a bit at the same time, even though the two places were worlds apart. I managed to avoid Tony for a few weeks but things came to a head around the end of July. He was in the pub one night when I went to meet Fran and when he went to the toilet he left his mobile on the bar. Fran and I started messing around with it and we found all these pictures of me. There were photos of me lying on his sofa, as well as pictures of between my legs, and some of them had been taken on that very first night I went there. It turned out he had been showing them to people in the pub but no one had bothered to tell me about it, which was nice of them.

I deleted all the pictures immediately and felt absolutely horrified that all the blokes in the pub had basically seen me naked – and worse. I also found out that he had told everyone he'd slept with me that first night. It was only then that Fran and I started putting two and two together. During those times I had visited him on my own he had either been mixing the coke with something or putting something in my drink which was knocking me out, and then he was having sex with me. He probably thought it was consensual because I had agreed to go back to his house. No wonder I had always felt so grubby after I stayed there.

I know it sounds ridiculous and you wonder how the hell I can't have known, but even though he was a bit odd I honestly didn't think he was capable of doing something like that. He was just a bloke from the pub. I thought he was creepy but harmless. Fran hadn't known about any of what had been going on and I like to think that if she had she would have told me. But all the other people who I saw as my group of mates had kept quiet the whole time it was going on, which really, really upset me.

When Tony got back from the toilet I started screaming at him and I picked up his phone and smashed it on the floor. I got taken outside by several people from the pub and told to go home and calm down. Once again, everyone thought I was just some drugged up nutter, while Tony was some sweet guy who from the outside didn't look like he'd harm a fly. People thought the things I was saying were paranoid ramblings and no one listened to me, even though I know some of them knew that there was truth in them.

Fran asked around about Tony later that night and apparently some of the people in the pub knew that he was a dirty old man and that he'd lured other girls back to his flat in the past. But the only time anyone had warned me about what he was like was that first time I met him at the cigarette machine, when Fran told me to stay away. No one else had ever said anything about his darker side.

I also found out that he'd been accused of rape before, but again, that didn't seem to bother all the people who knew I was going back to his flat alone with him. I have no idea what he did to me during those times I went round there. I strongly suspected that he'd molested me, or worse.

I desperately wanted to go the police but I was terrified that they wouldn't believe me. I was worried that they would look at me and see a drug addict who was clearly happy to take coke from this man whenever it was offered. I thought everyone would say that it was my own stupid fault. And I had no evidence for the attacks anyway. It was basically his word against mine.

I think in Tony's twisted mind he thought he was in love with me. Looking back he always tried to stay in control and would only ever do one line of coke for every six he had given me. He must have liked seeing me so out of it and thinking that he could do whatever he wanted

My family had absolutely no idea that any of this was going on around this time and the first person I wanted to call when I found out about everything was my mum. My parents had tried so hard to help me over the past year or so but they had all but given up on me because of the appalling way I had treated them. I only called them about once a month and always made sure that I was lucid so they didn't suspect anything. Believe me, it wasn't easy to find those moments.

By complete coincidence Edward also started calling me again to see how I was, but I was too ashamed to speak to him so I never answered my phone. Still to this day I don't speak to him. We stay in touch by text, but I think it would be too difficult to see him, no matter how much I want to. If I had stayed at The Priory when he took me the Tony episode of my life would never have happened, and that thought horrifies me.

Chapter 19

ONE WEDDING AND AN (ALMOST) FUNERAL

I was full of self-hatred for putting myself in the situations that I had done with Tony and I totally blamed myself for everything that had happened to me. I would sit for hours on end drinking vodka, staring at the bare walls of my flat and thinking about what I'd let him do to me. One day I got myself so wound up about it that I went to the local Internet café, tracked down the place where he worked and sent a group email to everyone at his company telling them that he had raped me and taken pictures of me naked. I wanted everyone to know what he had done and also to warn other women who knew him. Again, he didn't go to the police, which is surely the first thing you would do if you were an innocent man?

By the end of July my mental state was the worst

it had ever been. I was still taking the Temazepan the doctor gave me, but they weren't numbing me like I needed them to. I was hearing voices in my head all the time – something that I still do sometimes now – and it was impossible to sleep without taking Valium every night. I also suffered from horrendous nightmares where my family would be hurt or I would be repeatedly attacked. Every time I closed my eyes I had these awful paranoid thoughts about things like people trying to break into my flat and hurt me, or even burning it down with me inside. It was like being in some kind of mental prison. I had no control over it whatsoever and I thought that if I didn't sort myself out I would end up in a mental institution. I used to scream when I was on a comedown. I'd literally sit in my bedroom and scream my head off and cry hysterically. I had always suffered from comedowns but in the past it had just involved me crying for my mum. I lost count of the amount of times people took my phone off me when I was high to stop me phoning my mum and asking her for help. Maybe if I had managed to call her one of those times all this would have come to an end a lot earlier on.

My comedowns got so bad that I started self-harming just to provide myself with some kind of release. The first time I did it I was at home feeling like death. I had borrowed some money off someone – I can't even remember who – to get myself enough coke to level myself out. But as soon as it started wearing off I felt like hell again. I was lying on my bed crying and smoking a cigarette and I became fascinated with the burning tip. I stared at it for a few seconds, then I took it and pushed it into the underside of my left forearm. It made a horrible singeing noise and the pain was incredible, but once the pain stopped the relief I felt was amazing.

After that, burning myself became a daily event and even though it was the height of summer, I had to wear long sleeved tops at all times to try and hide the burn marks. I used to be fascinated by how perfectly round the marks were and I would gaze at them constantly.

I also started to cut my arms with my kitchen knives. Again, I always felt this amazing release once the pain subsided and the bleeding started. It was like I was trying to get all the bad stuff and the negative feelings out from inside of me. One time I was feeling so wretched I broke a glass and tried to swallow it because I knew it would cut up my insides and potentially kill me, but I couldn't go through with it. I chewed it up in my mouth and cut the inside of my cheeks, but it was impossible for me to swallow it, thank God.

I barely went out at all around that time because I had no money. Any time I did bump into anyone they would tell me how awful I looked. Fran still came round every now and again but I was so miserable that even she got sick of me. Where was the fun in hanging round with someone whose idea of a good time was putting fags out on their arms? I felt like I had no one.

Somehow – and to this day I still don't know how – I managed to take out a bank loan. I came up with the idea of applying for one when I heard an advert on the radio and I filled out a form thinking there was no way they would give it to me. But incredibly, they did. It was only for about a thousand pounds but it was enough to get me out of trouble for a while. I had a family wedding coming up that I had promised my parents during one of my 'straighter' moments that I would go to, so I knew I had to look half decent.

The first thing I did was get my hair done so I looked a bit more like my old self. My roots were dreadful and my hair was lank where I hadn't been looking after it but a trip to the hairdressers made all the difference. I also bought a new outfit and even treated myself to some make up. I knew if I turned up looking as bad as I had been my mum would have frog marched me back to Wales and padlocked me in my bedroom.

I bought some coke to take to the wedding because I knew there was no way I could make it through without it, and I also took some amyl nitrate, also known as poppers, with me. Because I had all this money I decided to get a chauffer driven BMW down to Beaconsfield, where the wedding was taking place. I decided that would make a good impression on my family. I was wearing a long sleeved cardigan even though it was the middle of August and about 75 degrees so that I could hide the evidence of my self-harming. I couldn't have anyone seeing my scabs and scars.

It was the first time I'd seen any of my family for about eight months and my mum gasped when she saw me. My brother looked me up and down and shook his head and then walked away. He didn't even say hello to me.

By early afternoon I knew I was acting quite irrationally as I'd already been drinking and had a couple of lines of coke, but I was doing my best to keep it together. People kept saying to my mum that I was acting strangely, which was clearly the case. I was talking ten to the dozen and laughing loudly at things that weren't even funny.

We all sat down for the wedding meal and I was put on a table with my mum, my cousins, my brother and his girlfriend. I got even more drunk and just before the speeches began I decided to announce to my entire table that I was a drug addict. To be honest, I had spent most of the day in the toilets and was sniffing constantly so people must have wondered what was going on anyway, but there was no need to be so blatant. My mum already suspected that I'd been doing drugs that day but she still looked shocked when I blurted it out, while all my brother could say was, 'I told you you were!' I also decided to tell everyone that I had been done for drink driving. I don't think my poor mum knew where to look. One of my cousins burst out laughing and then the whole table went quiet. I suddenly felt really awkward so just as the first speech started I legged it upstairs to do another line knowing that no one else would be able to follow me while the speeches were going on.

Somehow during the course of the day someone stole a gram of coke out of my bag, which I was absolutely furious about. There was another girl there who looked like a druggie and I'm convinced it was her who took it. I swear, addicts can sniff out other addicts a mile away. Then again, it could have been a member of my family who took it because they were trying to protect me? I guess I'll never know.

One of my male cousins tried to talk to me about drugs and said, 'It may be cool to read the papers and see Kate Moss and Sophie Anderton doing drugs but it's not cool to do them.' He must have thought I was just a silly girl who was messing around with coke a little bit here and there to try and look like a 'proper' model. Little did he know how deeply I'd become immersed in it.

I was sharing a hotel room with my mum that night and after the reception she kept trying to talk

to me about my revelations at the table, but I was
so drunk that I got into bed and fell asleep half way
through the conversation. God knows how she must
have felt.

Not surprisingly my family were very off with me
the following day and everything was very awkward.
My mum asked me to go back to Wales to live with
her and my dad again for a while but I flatly refused
and walked off to get a train home. My parents kept
phoning me following the wedding but I didn't take
any of their calls. They kept threatening to come up
and see me but I sent them a text to say that I'd
just gone a bit over the top at the wedding because
I was drunk and I was just doing it to show off. I
assured them I was totally fine and it wasn't something I did regularly and they seemed to accept my
explanation.

My parents reached out to me so many times to
try and help. My mum was always texting me saying,
'We're here when you need us.' They even offered
to pay for me to go on holiday with them so I could
have space to sort myself out. Deep down they knew
I had a problem, but I was so stubborn it was impossible for them to help me if I didn't want to help
msyelf. I was also a grown woman, so what were
they going to do? Force me to return to Wales?

I virtually stopped answering my phone to anyone
except Fran and the dealers, who I still used pretty
regularly. The money from the bank loan was keeping

me going and I was in my own little drugs bubble. I was still self-harming and I'd experience these massive highs followed by massive lows. One morning I woke up and immediately snorted the only two grams of coke I had left in the house. But this time instead of giving me a high they just made me feel shabby and tired, and the comedown was one of the worst I'd ever had. I think my body had got to the point where it was starting to totally give up on me. The voices in my head were louder than ever and every time I closed my eyes I was seeing images that were like something out of a horror movie with people being killed, my family being harmed and people chasing me. I was having the worst paranoia episodes I had every experienced.

I looked in the mirror and started sobbing uncontrollably at what I had become. I looked disgusting. I had hit absolute rock bottom and I could see no way out of it. I felt like everyone seemed to be trying to make money out of me or using me to get drugs. And I had ostracised my family and Edward – the few people in the world who did actually give a shit about me.

I made a decision. I went to the shop at the end of my road and bought two bottles of wine and some paracetamol. Then I walked to the next shop and bought as many ibuprofen as I could. I went home and lay all the tablets out on my bed, then I downed them with the wine. I took all of the

Tamazepan I had as well, just to make doubly sure that the combination would have the desired effect.

I wasn't at all scared about dying. In fact, in some ways I thought it would be a relief. I didn't even think about the effect it would have on my family and friends, basically because I didn't think they would care. I felt like everyone had given up on me a long time ago. I had almost forced them to.

I texted Fran simply to say, 'Thanks for trying to help me,' as soon as I'd taken all the pills. She was at work at the time but not surprisingly she became really alarmed by my text. She knew that if I had done something stupid she wouldn't be able to get to me in time, so she panicked and called the police to get them to send someone round to my house. Two policemen had to break in through my bedroom window, and they found me lying on my bed dipping in and out of consciousness. I was also covered in my own sick which I could easily have choked on.

Fran had called Tony in a total state and said to him, 'I'll kill you if my best friend dies.' So unbelievably he turned up at my flat. He managed to get in and see me by telling the police that he was my friend. I was in a total daze but I still managed to shout at him to get the hell out. I was babbling incoherently to the police about him attacking me while we were waiting for an ambulance to arrive, but thankfully they listened to my ramblings and they arrested him there and then. He was taken off for questioning, while I was stretchered out and taken to St Mary's hospital. I had my stomach pumped and then I was put me on a drip. I felt numb but a very, very small part of me was also happy that I had survived and I felt like maybe – just maybe – I did have something to live for after all. There was this really sweet Korean nurse who used to come and talk to me all the time. On my second day there she said to me, 'Why do you want to kill yourself? You're too beautiful for all this.' Then she smiled at me and said, 'I've got a secret!' I looked at her and said, 'You're pregnant!' She nodded happily and said she was seven weeks and two days gone. It was a really strange moment but in those few seconds I felt like it could have been the beginning of a new life for me as well.

Two men from CID came to visit me the following day. They told me that they'd spoken to Fran and they knew all about what Tony had done to me. They said they believed he had raped me. Tony had told them that I was his girlfriend and I had consented to everything, which was obviously never, ever the case. Thank God Fran backed me up because otherwise I wouldn't have had a leg to stand on. The police kept Tony in a cell for a day while they interviewed him but he denied ever giving me drugs or sexually assaulting me. The minute he was released he went to Bar Below and told everyone in there what had happened, which I found very odd. Why would you want to tell people about something like that?

I was in the hospital for three days in all and not one person came to visit me. I put Fran down as my next of kin so that my parents wouldn't find out about my latest suicide attempt, but not even she bothered to come and see me. I felt very sad about the fact that I was all alone and I later found out that Fran was too busy gossiping down the pub about what happened to come and see if I was okay. I was grateful that she had backed up my story about Tony, but that seemed to be where her support ended. She loved the drama side of what was going on, but it seemed that she didn't genuinely care about me. It took that episode to make it hit home that these people I had been hanging out with for months weren't my real friends. Not one of them cared about me unless they were having fun and doing drugs with me, and I realised how much time I'd wasted on them.

I felt really empty and alone but the lovely pregnant nurse was the one who got me through. She was so positive and happy. Obviously I had no way of getting any drugs so I was left alone with my thoughts 24 hours a day. I was put on a very strong painkiller which was helping to keep me calm, but there was no way I couldn't reflect back on everything I'd been through and see what an idiot I'd been.

I had to go and see a psychologist while I was in the hospital and I got the feeling she just saw me as another druggie and she didn't offer me much help. I decided there and then that no one else was going to be able to make my life better but me. It was my choice whether I wanted to live or die and whether I wanted to make things better for myself. It wasn't up to anyone else, and by that point I didn't actually want anyone to help me. I was going to prove to myself how strong I could be.

When it was time for me to leave hospital no one came to pick me up so I had to get a taxi home on my own. Because I'd been carried out half conscious I didn't have my house keys with me, and the window the police had used had been boarded up so I had to smash another window to get in. Fran came round later that day acting all concerned and I think she genuinely felt really bad that she hadn't been to see me in the hospital. After that she hardly left my side for days. Apart from when she went to Bar Below.

The police told me in no uncertain terms that I had to get off the drugs if I wanted to see Tony convicted, and I wasn't allowed to go to Bar Below any more in case he was in there. They said that no one would listen to me unless I looked like I was making a conscious effort to sort myself out. I agreed; I knew they were right, and I wanted to see justice done not only for me, but also for all the other women he had attacked.

Chapter 20

HOME
DELIVERY

Thankfully, after coming close to killing myself yet again and getting myself into some horrendously dangerous situations I finally – *finally* – decided to try and kick my coke habit once and for all.

I stopped going to Bar Below altogether. In fact, I couldn't even walk past the place without getting a feeling of complete dread in my stomach. I also cut down on my drinking. I knew I wouldn't be able to stop everything completely straight away, but I was doing around five to six grams of coke and two or three bottles of wine a day at that time, so I decided to try and cut down slowly. The thing is, it's so hard to turn your back on something when it's so readily available, and also when certain people don't really want to see you give up. I got in touch with all of the dealers I had been using and told them in no uncertain terms not to contact me again. I made it clear that if I owed anyone money, I would clear any debts and then I wanted nothing more to do with them.

One of the dealers I had been buying drugs from for some time obviously panicked that he was going to lose such a good customer so he started coming around to my flat and offering me freebies. Of course he knew that once I had a line or two I would need more and I would go to him to buy it, so it made sense to him. He literally used to drive around the streets looking for me and sit outside my house waiting for me to come home. He would knock on my door and say, 'I've got shopping for you!' which was code for having drugs to give me. And as much as I wanted to slam the door in his face, when you're feeling terrible, if someone is offering you something for free that you know will instantly make you feel better, it isn't easy to say no.

I kept asking him to leave me alone but he would just laugh at me and wave a little packet of powder in front of my face. And every time, I gave in. One night when he knocked on my door I refused to answer. I begged him to stop coming round and I explained for about the tenth time that I was trying to get off the drugs. He just rolled his eyes and turned up the next day and started shouting through my letterbox saying he had a delivery for me.

I knew that if I had any chance of recovery I had to get him out of my life so I decided to take drastic action. I called up two male mates of mine that I'd been at school with who I knew I could rely on. They were very tough, fearless guys and as soon as I explained why I needed help they were in a car on the way to London.

The next day when the dealer arrived as usual they went out to speak to him. I looked out the window just in time to see them putting him into the back of their car. I have no idea what happened after that or what they did to him, but the next day his car was gone from outside my house and he never bothered me again. I know it's not a normal way to deal with a problem, but that wasn't a normal problem.

I did see the dealer a couple of times after that around Putney as he used to deal to several other people in the area, but he used to cross the road to avoid me and would look directly down at the floor. God knows what my friends threatened to do to him, but whatever it was, it worked.

It would be stupid for me to pretend that coming off drugs after all that time was easy. It wasn't. It was one of the hardest things I've ever had to do in my life, but also one of the most worthwhile. Had I not stopped when I did it's very likely I may not have been here to write this book. I was under no illusion that I would cut out the coke and booze, get myself a nice little job and live a simple, happy life, but I knew that getting off drugs was my only option if I had any hope of a future. I was aware that getting off the drugs alone was going to be like a full-time job in itself.

I still carried on drinking over the next couple of weeks but I went completely cold turkey with the coke. I searched my flat from top to bottom – not that it took long because I had so few possessions left – and I made sure there wasn't even the tiniest bit of coke left anywhere to tempt me.

I stayed in my flat for days on end on my own with my phone switched off so I wouldn't be tempted to fall back into my old ways. Fran came and knocked for me a couple of times but I didn't answer. I knew that even a few quiet drinks could be the catalyst for more months of misery.

Being without coke was absolute agony. As well as the physical pain and the longing, I had fits where I would scream and cry at the top of my voice. Anyone walking past my flat would have wondered what the hell was going on. I was also completely delusional a lot of the time and totally and utterly paranoid. Even more so than usual. Every little noise made me jump and I would lie in bed with the duvet covering me, shaking and praying that I would get through it. There were times when I thought that if I died in my sleep it would be a blessing. Even though I felt like hell I didn't want to kill myself, but I decided that if it was God's will to take me, then so be it.

The alcohol helped to take the edge off the withdrawal symptoms, and I was still using my reliable old friend Valium to help me get to sleep at night. There's just no other way I would have been able to do it. Even though I was completely exhausted, every time I closed my eyes I felt wide awake again. I was probably drinking about a bottle and a half of wine a day, which was manageable. I didn't get a bad hangover on that amount, and I wasn't getting so drunk that I was tempted to give into my drug cravings.

I had been off all drugs for a week and a half when Fran came around and shouted through the letterbox, 'Come on Amy, you haven't been out for ages. Let's go out and get pissed!' I decided that as I'd been so good I deserved a night out. I got ready and went with her to a quiet local pub where I knew there was no way I'd be able to get my hands on coke. Unless one of the 80-year-old men who regularly propped up the bar were secret dealers, and that seemed extremely unlikely!

Fran and I drank about six bottles of wine between us and I could barely stand up by the time we went to leave, and I was so wrecked that my coke cravings came back with a bang. Thankfully Fran didn't have any coke on her, but I virtually crawled home crying and texting everyone I knew asking if they had any drugs. Thankfully no one – not even the dealers – got back to me. I felt so relieved when I woke up the next morning. I could so easily have relapsed.

Now I was getting clean I was more desperate than I'd ever been to move away from Putney and all the bad memories and bad people, but I owed so much back rent on my place that I knew it would take me a while to pay all that off first. Even though I stopped going to Bar Below it's one of those places where you always see the same people around the area because it's so small. Everyone seemed to know what had happened between Tony and I so I was always getting stared at in the street. Of course Tony had told everyone that I was mad and a liar and that I used to work as an escort girl. And because I hadn't been in the pub defending myself most people took his side and no one wanted anything to do with me. The only person who knew for sure that Tony had attacked me was Fran, and although I thought of her as a really good friend – my best friend in some ways I guess – sadly I never felt like she was properly on my side. In fact, for all I knew she was still happily using Tony for his coke.

I found it increasingly hard being in my flat with all the horrible memories. Now that I was seeing things more clearly the whole place felt cheap and grubby, but I simply didn't have enough money to move. I'd wake up in the morning and feel like I was still trapped in that old, seedy world. Then the thing I had been dreading happened and it gave me a clear sign that it was time to get the hell out of Putney, some way, somehow.

I was walking to the local shop to get some food and I saw Tony walking across the other side of the road. I felt my legs start to give way and before I could hide he saw me. He slowly turned around, fixed me with a steely stare, and made this face that was like a mix between a smile and a leer. I was so shocked at seeing him that I wanted to burst into tears, but instead I held his gaze until he looked away, and then I ran all the way home with my legs shaking beneath me. I felt like I couldn't breath properly and my heart felt like it was about to explode. But I was also happy that I hadn't let him see me break down. I hadn't let him beat me.

I needed to have a break from everything so I decided to go back to Wales to see my family. I hadn't touched drugs for over two weeks and I knew it would do me good to take myself away from all temptation. I arrived back home wearing a baggy jumper and some jeans, and although I certainly wasn't the picture of health, hopefully I looked a lot more together than I had done at the wedding.

Mum opened the door, took one look at me and wrapped me up in a massive hug. I think she was relieved that I'd had finally come to my senses because it was clear that I was there to ask for help. It's funny because although I knew my family would be there for me whenever I needed them it wasn't something I'd ever felt like I could do before. It was a massive step forward for me and I think it was the one thing that made me realise I was truly on my way to getting better. I'd always tried to hide everything from those close to me before because I was ashamed of what I'd become, but now I was ready to be honest about everything.

I dumped my bags on the floor and Mum and I sat down to share a bottle of wine. Everything – and I mean *everything* – came tumbling out in one long stream of conciousness. I sobbed as I told her about the rapes, the extent of my drug addiction and my recent suicide attempt. I lifted up the sleeves of my jumper and showed her all the scars on my arms and she cried her eyes out, and I soon did the same. The scars had faded a bit but they were still quite red and angry and I think anyone who had seen them would have been shocked, let alone my own mother. I had never really let my mum see me cry before but I felt like I needed to be honest with her.

She said she was upset that I hadn't asked for help before, so I tried to explain as clearly as possible why I couldn't. Even when I had wanted to, people always convinced me it was a bad idea. I remember telling Fran once when I was feeling really low that I wanted to sort things out with my parents. She told the other people I did drugs with about it, and they said that I didn't need my parents any more and that they were my new family now. I truly believed that they cared about me at the time. How stupid of me.

I stayed back in Wales for five days in all and it really helped me to get some perspective on things. My mum tried to get me to stay on for a while longer but I needed to stand on my own two feet if I was going to get my life back on track. She still insisted that she helped me out, and for the first time ever I gratefully accepted. She was very clever about how she did it though. She'd give me just enough money to travel to job interviews and she bought my food shopping for me online, and also some new clothes. She never gave me cash because she was worried that I would be tempted to spend it on things I shouldn't have done, but she always made sure I was clothed and fed well. Both of my parents told me that I could go back home to live with them any time I wanted. But I was 25 by then and to me moving back home would have felt like I'd failed in some way. This time I was going to make London work for me.

As soon I got back to London I started looking for a job. I wanted to make my own money and I didn't care what I did. Well, within reason. I knew there wasn't much chance of me getting modelling work again so I went for random jobs that I saw advertised in the paper.

I landed an interview for a job that would involve working on the business side of a forensic laboratory in Teddington. When the woman interviewing me looked at my rather bare CV and asked why I hadn't had a job for so long, I was completely honest and said that I'd been a drug addict and I was now trying to get my life back together. Thankfully she was brilliant about it and said she was happy that she could be the one to give me a second chance. I couldn't believe it when I landed the job there and then. It was my first regular job for years and it gave me a real focus. Finally I had something to get up for every morning.

I decided that now I was clean again I wanted to start going out in the West End again, but this time I was going to do it drug-free. I didn't want to go back to my old haunts, but equally I didn't want to hang around in Putney or Camden where I could easily fall back in with the same old people.

I knew a guy called Annas who worked for a company called Met Parties. I had met him on a night out the previous year and he was a lovely guy. He was very straight down the line and I knew that I could trust him. I texted him to say hi and he invited me to a party at a club called Embassy, which is based just near Regent Street. I was really nervous about going but I knew it would be a totally different crowd of people to the one I used to hang out with.

I got all dressed up and for the first time in ages I actually liked what I saw when I looked in the mirror. I had put on a little bit of weight and I looked so much healthier. It felt funny getting the train into town completely sober, but it was nice to be able to walk into a club with a clear head for . . . well, probably the first time ever. It was really busy inside and I saw several people I knew but thankfully no one offered me drugs. It was as if they could tell I was different now.

I looked around and I saw girls who were like I used to be. They'd roll up to the door all fresh and excited and loving the fact they were on the guest list. Then older, more experienced guys would take them under their wing and give them drugs, and they'd have the time of their life for a while. Then you wouldn't see them for a while and they'd turn up looking healthier and a bit rounder having just come out of rehab. As soon as that happens, the playboys would move on to other girls. It's laughable; the guys get older and the girls get younger.

It's so horrible to watch. I've seen so many older guys pass drugs to these naïve young girls in clubs. They'll pass them a wrap of coke or give it to them in a note and the girls will take it because they want to fit in. They think that's what having a good time is all about. I want to go over there and whack the men and pull the girls away because sadly I know too well how it will all end.

I soon got know some new people in Embassy – some genuinely nice people who didn't do drugs – and I started going out once or twice a week. Although I drank, I never even considered touching anything else, and no one even talked about drugs around me.

A month or so after I started going out again I went along to the premiere of the film Click in Leicester Square. A friend I'd met at Embassy got invited so she asked me if I wanted to go with her, and it was packed with celebrities. Someone introduced me to Lee Otway, the ex-Hollyoaks actor who had just come out of Love Island at the time. He was very sweet but you could tell that he was very insecure and he was really trying to show off a bit. As soon as we met he kissed me on both cheeks and said, 'I'm a bit busy now love, I've got to go and do interviews, but I'll see you later,' as if I was really bothered about him spending time with me. All the press were queued up to speak to David Hasslehoff and Lee went and queued up behind him. I'm not sure that anyone really wanted to speak to him, but he looked so happy to be a part of the media throng.

The after party was a huge affair and I'll never forget glamour girl Alicia Duvall dancing on a table wearing a dress that didn't even cover her very skimpy thong. I didn't know wear to look. She was revealing practically everything. Lee got up on the table and started dancing with her, but when he spotted me he got down and walked over and asked for my number. He was very sweet and quite charming, and then he looked down at the scars on my arms and said to me, 'I can see you've got problems and I want to take you under my wing and look after you.' But he was about a foot smaller than me and I was thinking, 'How are you going to look after *me*? I feel like I should be looking after *you*.'

Lee told me he was going to go and hang out in the VIP area, but when he got to the entrance they wouldn't let him in. Adam Sandler, the star of the film, was surrounded by people but Lee still went up to him and moaned, 'Why can't I come in the VIP section? Chris Brosnan is in there and I'm the guy off the telly. I was in Soapstar Superstar.' He finally got in and later he sneaked me in too. We were both sitting with The Hoff and Adam drinking champagne and having a really good laugh. Adam was really funny and friendly, and The Hoff was exactly as you'd expect – loud and brash but a nice guy. There was also a journalist in there from one of the tabloids who was running around trying to eavesdrop on people's conversations in the hope of getting a story. I had met her once before and she turned round and said to me, 'I'll give you five grand for a kiss and tell on Hasslehoff. You'll have to properly sleep with him though, anything less than that isn't worth as much.' I was absolutely furious. She obviously thought that because I'd done a couple of kiss and tells before and it was well known that I'd had a drug problem, I'd be an easy target. She honestly thought that I would basically prostitute myself for a few thousand quid. I thought about chucking my drink over her but I decided it would be a waste of a drink, so I just turned my back on her. She soon got the message.

I had a good laugh with Lee and he called me a few days later and invited me to the launch of a club called Sound in Leicester Square. Kate Lawler was DJ-ing and there were quite a lot of celebrities going so it sounded like a laugh. Lee wasn't exactly the perfect gentleman and spent most of the night chatting up other girls while I did shots at the bar with one of his mates. But by the end of the night I was so drunk I ended up back at his house with him. He started getting really paranoid about me selling a story on him and was saying, 'I know the papers are out to get me. I know you're going to do a dodgy story on me.' But he still didn't ask me to leave. I wondered if maybe he secretly wanted me to sell a story on him so he'd get in the paper.

Lee put Snow Patrol's Run on his stereo and he kept singing it over and over for about an hour. He was very drunk but I still thought it was very bizarre and in the end I had to beg him to stop. It was driving me mad. We stayed up talking until about 4am and I stayed the night with him, but nothing really happened between us. He was a sweet bloke but in a way he seemed even more screwed up than I was. In fact, the next time he invited me round to see him I knocked on his door and he came running out shouting, 'Where are the paps, where are the paps?' I'd only gone round because I'd had a few drinks and wanted to say hello, so I was very taken aback. I wasn't interested in selling a story on him and I thought we were mates. It was all ridiculous.

I bumped into him a few times after that but nothing ever happened between us again. We liked each other a lot but there was no romance there. He was like a little kid who needed his ego stroked, and I didn't have the energy for it. I wanted someone who would take care of me, not someone I had to look after and tell them they were wonderful all the time.

I started going to Embassy pretty regularly during the week and I met some really nice people who, for the first time in a while, I felt weren't out to use me. For the first time in ages, I felt happy. I hadn't done any drugs for over two months and I'd managed to cut back completely on the alcohol. I now only drank when I went out, never at home, and I even stopped keeping booze in the house so I wasn't tempted to start again. I also got back in touch with a girl called Emily, who I knew in my early modelling days. I knew that she had been through similar addiction problems to me and that she'd got through it, and she was such an inspiration to me. She used to call me every day to make sure I was okay and she kept encouraging me to stay off the drugs. We'd meet up and go out for drinks or I'd go round and visit her and her son, and I feel like she was really integral in me staying true to my word to stay on the straight and narrow. She recently moved to New York and I was so sad to see her go. We're still in touch but I miss her every day and I'll never forget how much she helped me.

I stayed in touch with my family a lot more as well and I felt much more connected to them. I think drink and drugs can make you very insular and I felt like I wanted to be a proper part of my family again, and thankfully they were very forgiving about everything that I'd put them through.

Sadly my partying soon got me into trouble again. I woke up after an evening at Embassy to find that I had chronic cystitis. I had to take a couple of days off work to recover, but when I went back I was called in to the boss's office and told that I'd been spotted at Embassy the night before I'd taken a sick day. She refused point blank to believe that I had been genuinely ill and I was sacked on the spot. I was so disappointed; I had felt really proud of myself when I got the job so it was a real let down.

I could have got quite down and angry about what happened but instead I picked myself up and looked around for another job. I soon got work temping with a recruitment agency and the run up to Christmas ran pretty smoothly. I was still plotting my escape from Putney, but in the meantime I went home to my parents' house for Christmas. My behaviour could still be quite erratic and because I was so excited to be home mum said that there were times when I was like a wind-up doll. I'd have these brief hyperactive moments as if someone had turned a huge key in my back, and then all of a sudden I would slump on the sofa looking very tired. I was definitely very up and down.

I admit I did drink quite a lot over those few days, but on Christmas Day I silently celebrated the fact that I had managed to stay clean from drugs for three and a half months.

My mind also wandered to Tony, who I knew would be spending Christmas Day on his own, as he did every year. When I looked around at my family, I realised how lucky I was to have them. Whatever Tony had done to me didn't matter that day. He was the one who was miserable; probably sitting at home doing lines of coke and hoping that the doorbell would ring and someone would come and keep him company. I knew that once the court case came up my life would be thrown into turmoil again knowing I had face him, but in the meantime I was the one who was, bit by bit, getting my life back together. I had even met a nice man who I really hoped I could have a future with.

I first got introduced to this guy I'll call Mike while I was at a party in Embassy. He was a footballer, although it took me a while to recognise him because although in his heyday he had been incredibly good looking, he had put on a lot of weight and he looked vastly different. He was wearing this really cool brown suit and I could tell that he was high so at first I stayed away from him. But once we got chatting I discovered that he was a really lovely guy. He gave me his number and I texted him shortly afterwards and we started speaking regularly. I knew it wasn't the best idea to be around someone who was into drugs, but equally it seemed like the ultimate test for me. And besides, there was something about him I really liked.

I was lying in bed one morning at about six o'clock and I texted Mike saying that I couldn't sleep. He texted straight back saying that he'd been up for hours too and he invited me over. I knew in the back of my mind that if he was anything like I had been when I was on drugs he would probably have been up all night. I was desperate for company so I jumped in a cab and headed over to his flat. Nothing happened between us but we laughed a lot and cuddled up on the sofa watching TV. It felt really natural, as if we'd known each other for years. He was doing coke while I was there but incredibly I wasn't in any way tempted to do any. People were constantly telling me how much better I was looking and I felt like a different person, and I knew I didn't ever want to go back to my old ways again.

Mike and I met up a few more times and I soon found out that he was a lot like I had been just a few months before. He was suffering from depression and he was doing a lot of coke to level himself out. We were like two lonely people who had found each other and we really liked each other's company. At first nothing happened between us and we were just like friends for a couple of weeks, but then he started to send me really sweet, romantic texts and poems when we were apart, and things soon progressed. We were like best friends with benefits. The benefit being that we were always there for one another and it was so nice having someone to look after me.

We became incredibly close really quickly. But the closer we got, the more of a problem the drugs became. He was every bit as bad as I had been at my peak, and when I went round he'd sit in front of his living room table, sieve the cocaine onto a book and snort line after line in front of me. I hated seeing the state he got into and it started to make me feel increasingly uncomfortable.

The one good thing was that he knew all about my past and he was very protective of me when it came to drugs. He always warned me off them and said that if I ever touched them again we'd be over. Ironic, really. He admitted that he even tested me once by leaving a huge pile of coke in front of me while he popped out to the off-license, but once it was out of my system I simply didn't want it back in there, so I didn't touch a bit.

The more Mike and I saw of each other, the more I knew there was no way things could work out. I liked him so much and he was such a great guy but I couldn't sit there night after night and watch him destroy himself like I'd nearly destroyed myself. I tried to talk to him about the drugs numerous times, but like I did, he had to get to the place where he actually *wanted* to give up and wanted to be helped, and he definitely wasn't there yet.

It got to the point where I told him that I had to stop seeing him. I admitted that I was terrified that one day I would turn up to see him and he would be dead. He was such a mess most of the time and it was sad to see because at one time he had been at the top of his game, so to speak. I begged him one last time to stop but he wasn't ready to and there was no way I could convince him. I told him that I would always be there for him but I couldn't stand to watch what he was doing to himself. We lay for hours together on the sofa as we always did and eventually we fell asleep. But when morning came I hugged him goodbye and told him that even though I cared for him a great deal, I couldn't see him any more.

Even though I hadn't been in touch with anyone from newspapers for ages there were *still* a couple of journalists sniffing around and trying to make money from me. One girl in particular, a girl from Manchester, we'll call her Jane, had always been really bad about hassling me to tell her what was going down on the party scene and who was up to what. There are always a lot of celebrities on the scene and so you always got to see them misbehaving. Jane had my mobile number and even though I had asked her to stop calling me several months before, she'd still phone me every now and again and ask me if I had any stories for her. It's the way freelance journalists who work for newspapers make their money; they'll get the story from you, sell it for a fortune and then give you a small cut and pocket the rest themselves. No wonder they're so desperate for you to spill the beans.

Jane had heard on the grapevine that Mike and I had become friendly. I guess because people had seen us at Embassy with each other and journalists have what they called 'contacts' – people who sell them stories – everywhere, someone had mentioned it. She called me up and started piling on the pressure telling me that I had to do a kiss and tell otherwise she was going to run the story in one of the papers anyway and make me look really bad. When I refused to tell her anything she started shouting down the phone, 'How the f**k do you expect to make any money when you won't do a kiss and tell you stupid bitch?' I told her never to call me again or I'd report her to all the newspaper editors, and then I put the phone down on her before she could answer. I was disgusted at how she'd acted, and that call made me realise that now I wasn't a druggie, I didn't have to deal with people like her any more.

I thought that was the last I'd hear of her but a friend of mine called me the following say and told me that Jane had been hawking my story around all the tabloids saying that she had a 'shocking and exclusive' story about Mike and I. What the hell was she going to tell people? About how we spent nights cuddled up together on his sofa chatting? The fact that Mike did drugs wasn't a major secret and there was no other story to speak of. I just laughed and said that I wished her luck because she was going to have a hard job selling something that didn't exist. Needless to say, nothing ever got printed.

Chapter 22

HIT
AND RUN

They say that money can buy you everything, and I found that to be true when the police called me at the end of January 2007 to say the case against Tony had collapsed. He had hired this hugely expensive solicitor who has worked on a number of very famous, high profile cases. The solicitor had done a lot of digging on me and managed to track down the magazine magazine piece I'd done on Carl, and also the tabloid story about John Leslie. Apparently the Criminal Prosecution Service were less than impressed. My past had well and truly come back to haunt me. I guess if you've already been given a label of some kind it's very hard to shake it off. All of those stories painted me in a very bad light and I was seen as a completely unreliable witness.

I was devastated and I blamed myself for everything all over again. I cried and cried; furious that

Tony would never be brought to justice. But once I finally stopped crying I felt a strange sense of release. It made me see how wound up I had been feeling while I waited to find out if the case was going to court, and now I knew for sure that it wasn't happening it meant that I could move on with my life. But before I did, I felt like I had to get my revenge on someone who had well and truly betrayed me.

One night when I was walking home after a night out I saw a guy who had worked in Bar Below when I used to hang out there. I knew he had lied about what had happened between Tony and I and that he knew a hell of a lot more than he let on to the police. He was another part of the reason that the case had collapsed, even though when the case had first come to light he had told me that he would back me up. Because I'd had a little bit of Dutch courage I walked over and punched him square in the face twice, and then said, 'That's for lying,' to him. He reported it and one Sunday afternoon while I was lazily watching EastEnders the police knocked on my door and arrested me.

Bizarrely, rather than have a go at me, the police seemed to think it was funny. On the way to the police station one of them asked me what I did for a living and when I said I'd done modelling he laughed and said, 'You'll be doing community service with Naomi Campbell next!' We then drove past Bar Below and the same police officer joked,

'Smile and wave!' So we all did. It was like it was all some kind of joke.

I was told I had been arrested for common law assault and when we got to the station I was so shocked by it all that I burst out laughing. The police sergeant was furious and said, 'Seeing as you find it so funny we're going to put you in a cell.' I was placed in this tiny, cold, dingy little cell. It was my own silly fault for laughing but they were blatantly just making a point, and it wasn't like I was dangerous or anything. I found it all pretty ridiculous.

A couple of hours later the duty solicitor turned up all guns blazing to represent me. She took me into an interview room and said to me, 'They've got no evidence but I can't help you if you lie about anything.' I wasn't about to turn around and admit everything if they had no evidence, so I told her that she may as well leave. I asked one of the officers if I could please have another phone call – I had used my first one to call Fran and ask her to give me an alibi – and thankfully they let me. I phoned Mike and explained what had happened and asked him if he could help me. He immediately sent me down a solicitor that he'd used in the past, who was amazing. He was so sharp and on the ball and said to the police, 'What my client is saying is that this guy has clear motivation for making this story up. You've got no evidence and no facial injuries, so either bail my client or charge her.' In the end they had to let me go, which was such a relief.

I went straight over to Mike's house to say thank you and when he asked if I was guilty I nodded. He was really angry with me and said that he was going to take me back down to the police station. In Mike's mind he was convinced that if they knew I had punched the guy it would have looked like I was telling the truth about Tony all along, and that's why I'd had such good reason to do it. He also thought that it made me look like a better person than Tony and all his friends because at least I'd had the guts to admit what I'd done, while they'd all lied.

Ridiculously he frog marched me back down to the station – I still to this day can't believe I went with him – and we spoke to one of the officers who had arrested me. Mike told him I was guilty but he just shrugged and said, 'I know that, but at the end of the day there was no evidence, and sometimes the law does not go in favour of the victim. Now, get lost you two.' We walked out and Mike turned to me and said, 'At least I tried,' but I could tell he was still really angry with me.

That was the last time I saw Mike because he stopped going out to the same clubs I did and we stopped calling each other. I heard through some friends a while later that he had given up the drugs, and he had admitted that it was an ex-girlfriend who made him wake up to what he was he doing to himself and effectively saved his life. He didn't give her name so I don't know if it was me or not, but whoever it was I'm so glad that he managed to sort himself out because he truly was a lovely person. He's even back playing football again, which was always his goal, if you'll pardon the pun. It makes me smile when I see pictures of him now because he looks like his old self again and I feel really proud of him. He deserves to be happy.

Now I had beaten the drugs another problem came back to haunt me – my weight issues. The drugs had always kept me really thin, but I put on weight very quickly once I started to eat normally again. My appetite returned with a vengeance and I guess where my body had been so starved of nutrients it was now craving food in a bid to replace everything it had lost. I was so physically weak at the height of my addition that there were days I found it hard to walk as I was so undernourished, and now my body loved the fact that it was being looked after.

As a result of my food cravings I put on almost two stone in the run up to Christmas and during the course of January. As much as I had hated being skinny, all of a sudden I found myself feeling fat, even though realistically I probably just looked healthy. Looking back it wasn't just about the weight though, it was also to do with control. When I was on the drugs I felt like I was in control of myself, when in reality of course I wasn't. But when I was off them I think I needed something else to focus on and my weight became that thing. I would be absolutely fine if I ate healthy food, but every time I ate something I deemed to be 'junk food' I would go to the nearest toilet and make myself sick.

I thought I was being really careful and clever about it, but people soon started to notice so I clearly wasn't as cunning as I thought I was. But in a way that was a blessing because it made me come to my senses pretty quickly and within a couple of months I was able to stop doing it. I didn't seek any help or anything, I decided that I needed to be strong enough to do it on my own. And thankfully, I was.

I carried on doing temping jobs here and there for the next few months. It was mainly reception work and it was quite dull, but it filled the time and it meant that I would soon have enough money to move to a new flat. All my back rent was nearly cleared so it wouldn't be long before I could move.

I was looking at MySpace during my lunch hour at work one day and I saw I had a message from a guy I used to know called Phyllis. He was a rugby player that I'd met at the London Wasps. He was a really nice guy and he had a massive heart and lovely blue eyes. We started messaging each other and then he asked me out for a drink. I was a bit nervous about dating again after Mike as part of me still really liked him, but I didn't think it could hurt.

We arranged to meet up but – sod's law – the day we were due to meet I was having a really bad day and I had a bit of a relapse. I don't know what caused it but I found myself in a pub at opening time with a double vodka in my hand. I went to meet Phyllis at the Millennium Hotel in Mayfair later in the day. He had been having a business meeting there and when I arrived I was already absolutely hammered. We went on to a bar nearby and the PR for the bar recognised Phyllis so she sent a bottle of champagne over to our table. We ended up having another two bottles and I could barely stand up by the end of the night. Phyllis must have wondered what on earth he was doing there with me. The last time he saw me I was a health conscious athlete, and here I was downing booze and smoking constantly At one point he said he felt sad about how my life had turned out. I guess he expected me to achieve a lot more considering my background.

I remember staggering to the bathroom and throwing up at one point, then coming back to the table and having more champagne. What a hot date! Not surprisingly, that was our first and only date. We did keep in touch and although he said he liked me, he knew I wasn't girlfriend material as I was still so all over the place. He lived abroad as well so we could only ever keep in touch by phone or text, which made things really difficult.

I think even now I'm really hard to have a relationship with. When it comes to guys I'm a bit of a wreck. I just don't trust anyone. Unless they've been in my past for a long time and I know them really well, I find it very hard to let them into my future. I only agreed to go out with Phyllis because I knew him. I turned down drinks with plenty of other guys along the way, simply because I don't want to get involved with users again, in any sense of the word.

Last year I started seeing a guy I'll call Snakehips. Again the only reason I agreed to the date was because I had known him when I was a teenager because he knew Gavin Henson through work. He admitted to me that Gavin had really slagged me off to him and called me a psycho, but Snakehips said that even he could see that I was a bit nuts; he got past that and saw the girl on the other side. I thought that was a really sweet thing to say; especially when I think back to our first disastrous date in the late spring of 2007.

I was back in Cardiff for my mum's birthday and Snakehips asked me if I wanted to go for some lunch. I met him in this bar and proceeded to make my way through two bottles of champagne. By the time he had dropped me home I was completely plastered and it was only about four o'clock in the afternoon.

He came into my house with me to make sure I got in safely. I had already flung my shoes off in the car and I was laughing my head off at everything he said, so I was acting a bit irrationally to say the least. My mum was furious when she saw how drunk I was as we were supposed to be going out for dinner that evening, so she told me to go and lie down and sober up. But instead I went outside, flagged down a passing car and asked the two young guys driving to drop me off at Snakehips's house as I could vaguely remember where he lived.

The boys clearly thought I was some kind of nutter, but they agreed to drop me off when I told them that Snakehips was a famous rugby player! When I arrived Snakehips's dog was running around in the garden so I knew I had the right house, but he was nowhere to be seen. The house was unlocked so I let myself in and went into his kitchen. About five minutes later he walked in to find me sat there shoeless in his kitchen, swinging my legs about like a child. He gave me a coffee, texted my parents to let them know that I was safe and then put me into the bed in the spare room. Thankfully he found it all quite funny and we did see each other again quite a few times and we were even properly seeing each other for a while. I used to go home most weekends to see him, which meant that I could get away from London. Things fizzled out after a while but we stayed in touch and we're still good friends now. In a lot of ways he gave me my confidence back because he could see that there was more to me than the insecure girl many other people saw.

Chapter 23

WHAT A SHAMBLES

The summer of 2007 was one of my strangest and most fun ever. I had regained my zest for life and I made a really nice new friend called Jenny, who I met at Embassy. She called me and invited me to the 02 Wireless Festival in Leeds. She was a singer and her agent had managed to get her VIP passes so we were so excited. There were loads of celebrities there from Coronation Street and Emmerdale, as well as quite a few pop stars. All the drinks were free so I was like a kid in a sweet shop. I was still being very careful not to have alcohol in my flat, but whenever I went out I still liked to get really drunk and I just never really knew when to stop.

From the moment we arrived there I was throwing drinks down my neck as quickly as I could get them from the bar. I was talking to a gorgeous guy from Emmerdale for ages and we were getting on really well, but then he stormed off because he saw a girl he fancied from the show getting off with another guy, so that was the end of that.

I remember that Chris Moyles kept staring at my legs and saying how nice they were. A while later I was sitting on my own at a table and this really drunk roadie came over and tried to pull me out of my chair and kiss me. Chris Moyles came over and asked him to leave me alone, and I returned the favour by slurringly telling him his radio show was shit. I really don't have any kind of 'stop' switch when I'm drunk and I did feel bad when I sobered up. Thankfully he was very sweet to me though and he just laughed and told me to have another drink, which I did.

I spent the whole weekend drunk and only managed to go and see one band, Daft Punk, and I don't even remember that very well. I must have passed out in the backstage bar about ten times over the course of the two days, but every time I came to I would go back to the bar and get another glass of wine. At one point some of the event ambulance people saw me pass out on the grass and tried to stretcher me off, but one of the bar men came running over and told them not to bother. He said that I'd been passing out all weekend and I was fine. Apparently they looked at me, rolled their eyes and walked off. I only found out about the episode later when someone relayed the story to me and I found it absolutely hilarious.

I managed to get through the whole weekend without taking drugs, even though I was offered a lot. I knew I would have to get a handle on the booze at some point, but I decided not to try and do everything at once. Well, that was my excuse. I guess I still needed some kind of prop.

I got a bit of a taste for festivals after going to the O2, so when someone offered me VIP tickets to V Festival in Chelmsford a couple of weeks later I nearly ripped their arm off I was so excited. Again, the plan was just do drink and not touch drugs. But not all plans work out as they should and I managed to do five Es over the course of the weekend.

I'd never been a big fan of Es and had only ever done them a few times, but the person who gave them to me guaranteed that they were good ones. Thankfully he was right and before I knew it I was floating around the VIP area with a massive grin on my face. I remember being in this tent and lighting a cigarette, and the next minute the whole place looked like it was full of stars.

I went out to see Babyshambles play with some friends and I remember thinking that it was absolutely magical at the time, but I couldn't actually remember much about the set afterwards. It seems a bit pointless looking back!

Afterwards I decided that I absolutely had to meet Pete Doherty. I had always been a fan and I had a massive crush on him. Somehow I managed to convince the bouncers who were guarding the backstage area that I was a journalist and I was due to interview him, so they let me through. I saw him standing around talking to some people and I rushed over to say hello. I asked him if he was still dating Kate and he smiled at me and said, 'Kate who?' He was wearing a Union Jack flag and he looked really sexy. He bent over and kissed me on the cheek and the next thing I knew we were snogging. Another member of the band, shouted at us both to 'get a room' and I laughed my head off. Pete was nothing like he's portrayed to be. He was really charming and friendly, and after we finished kissing I gave him a big smile and slowly wandered off back to the main VIP area feeling like I was walking on air.

Later in the evening I was queuing for the toilets when this very famous female TV presenter came out of the ladies right in front of me and gave me a big smile. When I went into the loo she had left me a massive line of coke. It was such a crazy thing to do because I could have been anyone. Imagine if I was a journalist? But she was obviously pretty out of it and I later saw her being carried back to her Winnebago by one of her male co-stars, who was clearly keen to get her away from all the press who were circling around.

You may find this hard to believe, but I didn't do the line. I felt like it would cheating. I knew that Es weren't something I would ever do regularly, but I was aware that all it would take was one line to send me careering back into some kind of addiction, which was the last thing I wanted.

I was with some friends who knew Erin O'Conner so we got introduced and she was so beautiful in the flesh and so normal and down to earth. Unlike Lily Allen, who pushed in front of me in the queue to get food and was acting like a total diva. She was with a bouncer and the pair of them were literally pushing everyone aside. Everyone was moaning loudly but she didn't seem to care. Then as she walked away from the food area she spat on Peaches Geldof. I have no idea why, but everyone was talking about how vile Lily was.

Kate Moss was also being a real diva. She tried to get everyone kicked out of one of the VIP areas so her and her friends could have some privacy, but she was told where to go. I don't know how or why but I heard she also made Sarah Harding from Girl's Aloud cry that day, which was a real shame as she seems like a sweet girl. It's shocking how celebrities get so above themselves. They're only human at the end of the day, no matter how rich or beautiful they are.

In the cold light of day I was annoyed that I had done drugs and I felt horrendous when I got home after the weekend. I knew instantly that I had no desire to do it again. It had been fun at the time but

I was really suffering for it, so it wasn't at all worth it. I had been feeling pretty levelled out but the Es made me dip into depression for a good few days again, and it reminded me how awful that felt.

On a more positive note, I had finally saved up enough money to move flats and I was so happy. All I needed to do now was find somewhere to live. And thankfully I soon found the perfect place and the perfect flatmate. I was invited to a party at the home of Julian Bennett, who is a TV presenter I'd met in Embassy. At first I didn't want to go because I was still completely paranoid about going round to the houses of people I didn't know very well. I still didn't really trust anyone that I hadn't known for a long time so I said thanks, but no thanks. Julian was really insistent and said to me, 'You've got nothing to worry about darling. For a start the party is for charity so it's not like anything untoward is going to go on, and secondly it's going to be full of gay men.' That convinced me I should go. It sounded like a lot of fun!

I soon found out that I definitely made the right choice. The party was great and everyone was so friendly. It also felt like a huge step in the right direction that I had managed to go to someone else's house and feel comfortable. I was happily tucking into the wine and chatting away to everyone. Chico from The X Factor was there and I kept bellowing, 'It's Chico time,' at the top of my voice. I thought

I was really funny, but the poor guy obviously hears it all the time, but he was friendly and he was humouring me and laughing along.

I was standing with a group of guys and we were all messing about when I shouted out, 'I need a gay best mate!' Suddenly this guy came running up from the bottom of the garden waving his hands in the air and saying, 'Me, me! Pick me!' His name was Armand and he was really handsome and charasmatic. He was very camp, and when we started talking I found out that he had just finished college and he was living in a place in Westminster. We clicked straight away.

We spent the rest of the evening gossiping and laughing and when the time came to leave we exchanged numbers. We arranged to meet up soon afterwards and we got on brilliantly. We started hanging out loads and a few weeks later he asked me if I wanted to move in with him as he had a spare room. I didn't need to be asked twice. We literally went to my place in Putney there and then in his car, put my stuff in black bin bags and left.

It felt amazing to be out of Putney. I hadn't been out around there for months, and thankfully I'd managed to avoid seeing all the people I used to hang out with at Bar Below. All I did was go to and from work every day, and then at the weekends I'd go into town to a club. I saw Fran very occasionally and we kind of pretended to be friends, but I couldn't get over how badly she had treated me at times. I felt like moving away would also give me a chance to break ties with her completely, and I was so glad.

Chapter 24

CROSSING THE FINISHING LINE

Moving in with Armand felt like another fresh start for me and like I could close the Putney chapter of my life. My mum came down and helped me to settle into my new place and it was so nice to be somewhere that actually felt like home. Armand made me feel so welcome. He was always cooking for me and making sure I was okay and within weeks we had become virtually inseparable.

I had still been taking my anti-depressants, but after a month of being in my new place I finally felt as if it was safe to come off them. I did it really slowly and gently so I didn't have a huge crashing low and I did feel like it was the right time to do it. I definitely felt a little bit more panicky being off them, but I also felt relieved that I wasn't having to rely on anything any more.

A few months later my transformation from messed up druggie to a normal, healthy member of society felt like it was complete when I was booked for a fashion show. I was looking a lot healthier and a friend in the industry recommended me for the Clothes Show Live at the NEC in Birmingham. Peaches Geldof was hosting and it didn't feel at all pretentious like some of the other shows I did. There were also no drugs around, which was a refreshing change. It made me wish that all the modelling jobs I'd done had been like that. Maybe if they had been I wouldn't have ended up the way I had, but who knows?

The clothes were really beautiful, and for the first time in a long while I did feel like the fashion industry was quite glamorous. Some of the other girls looked so gorgeous and I felt self-conscious when I turned up with my hair tied back, no make up and self harm marks on my arms. But later, once my make-up and hair had been done, I looked at myself in the mirror and thought 'wow.' I almost looked back to how I had done before living to excess had taken its toll on me. The telltale signs of addiction were still evident to those who looked for them, but I couldn't stop smiling when I saw how good I looked.

I spent Christmas 2007 back with my family and it was the first time in years that I had truly enjoyed myself. I didn't drink excessively and I was able to have conversations with my family without shouting or crying or being crazily up and down, which was quite a breakthrough. I even stayed in on my own for New Year as I didn't feel like going partying. I could see the main Central London fireworks from my flat and it seemed like the perfect way to end what had been a very mixed year. The beginning had been hellish, but the past six months had been much more positive and I felt like there had been a huge shift in my life. I was able to make clear, lucid decisions about what I wanted for myself, and as I stood there along watching the sky light up, I knew for sure I would be okay. I didn't cry, I didn't reflect too much on the past few years and the mistakes I'd made, I just looked to the future.

The next day I had lunch with my friend Emma-Louise and her son, and I couldn't think of anyone else I'd rather have spent the day with. We just looked like two friends chatting and having fun, and that's just how I felt. No drama, no drugs, just a nice, quiet, normal lunch.

My life now is so much quieter and I'm more of a home girl than a nightclub girl. I still go out sometimes to bars in London, but I haven't been to any of my old haunts for a long, long time. Now instead of going out all night I'll go out for dinner with friends. And when I drink champagne, I mix it with orange juice to dilute it so I don't totally ruin the evening by being drunk and forgetting half of it. I no long feel the need to spend a large proportion of my life off my head. I spent the best part of my early 20s drunk and it seems like such a waste.

I'm not going to pretend that everything is amazing now because of course there are repercussions from the drug years. There are still days now when I can't get out of bed because I'm so depressed, and I'm sure that's something that will always stay with me. Luckily my friends now know the way I am so they're there for me in a way that people haven't been before, and I always tell myself that after every low there will be a high.

As an athlete, when I got an injury I would see a physiotherapist; he would help me repair the damage that I had caused and give me something to ease the pain. But when my life broke down and my heart was broken, there was no science or doctor to fix it, I just had to try and feel my way through. My emotional breaking point after the abortion was a weakness I had never experienced before, and I didn't know how to handle it, hence I spun totally out of control.

I've made a lot of mistakes in my life and I've learnt my own lessons. For a long time I dismissed the possibility of getting my life back on track, thinking I wasn't capable of doing it and it was too hard to contemplate. But there came a point where I couldn't be who I was – an addict – any longer. It was do or die. I've now learnt that walking slowly to the finish line is better than never finishing at all. Even the worst failure is better than never trying.

I still remember the fairy tale bedtime stories my parents told me when I was a little girl. The shoe fit Cinderella, the frog turns into a prince and Sleeping Beauty gets awakened by a kiss. It was all so magical. The dreams I had for myself when I was younger turned out a little differently than I expected. Instead, my nightmares became my reality. Prince Charming never came riding on a white horse to rescue me, and the castle I had fantasised about became a seedy nightclub or a drug-filled penthouse apartment.

I went to the doctor recently to see about having my self-harm scars lasered away, but when I spoke to my mum about it afterwards she suggested I leave them. She said to me, 'Amy, it's up to you and you need to do whatever makes you happy, but you did the self-harming for a reason, and you must never forget the reason why. Those scars will always remind you that you don't want to go back to that place again.' That's so true. They're what I was; not what I am or what I will ever be again.

I never, ever set out to be famous or a celebrity but I'm more than aware I've been branded 'notorious' by some people. Now I just want to be able to put my head on my pillow every night and know that I did my best that day. I believe that you can choose to be a victim and you can choose to let someone else change your life, but I made the choice to get my life on track. Loads of people have asked me how I've managed to stay sane throughout everything, but I have good and bad days like everyone else. I still have times where I will down a bottle of wine in one go just to get a bit of a release, but those times are so few and far between now.

I admit that I am still angry with the way some people treated me when I was at my lowest. At the end of the day, I took drugs. That was my fault and nobody else is to blame for that. I take full responsibility for the state I ended up in. But what I'm angry about is the way that people used me when I was vulnerable. Especially people who I considered to be my friends. I have broken ties with nearly everyone from the bad old days now. I think that if they weren't good for me then, they're definitely not good for me now.

I'm also angry with the people who, for whatever reason, didn't want me to recover. Those people who took my phone off me when I wanted to call my parents, or the ones who turned up to my AA meetings 'for a laugh'. Apart from my parents, Edward was the only person who ever really tried to help me. He threw me a lifeline when he sent me to rehab but I wasn't ready to be helped. Because no matter how much the drugs were hurting and destroying my life, the thought of letting go and facing up to reality hurt even more. But I won't forget Edward for as long as I live. He's an incredibly kind, special man.

Constantly chasing a high made everything else in my life fade away. It's incredible to think how much I humiliated myself, and how much other people used that humiliation as entertainment. Even though some of the tabloids knew I had a drug problem they would still happily give me money in exchange for a story about my sad, shameful life. To them I was a cash cow; someone to be used to make money. And they made themselves feel better about it by throwing a bit of money my way as well, which ultimately they knew would be sucked up my nose.

I recently signed with a new agent and he's turned down more work than he's taken on for me as he doesn't want me to do anything that will be bad for me. His interest is my wellbeing. I'm working with people I trust, possibly for the first time ever. One thing I'm better at now is working out who is out for themselves and who is good for me to be around. I'm sure I'll still make mistakes here and there, but hopefully not as bad as the ones I have made in the past.

It's weird when I look back on everything that has happened to me. It's like I'm looking at someone else's life. I was all set to be a serious athlete and two bad incidents sent me down a dark and dangerous path. I must have been quite a weak person though, as I allowed everyone to lead me astray. Part of me must have wanted to do those things. I have to take responsibility for all of my actions, if not for all of the things that happened to me along the way as a result of them.

I do worry about the long-term effects the drugs will have on me as I guess we still don't know just how damaging they can be. They've definitely made me more paranoid and unable to trust people, but I'm hoping that because my body is young it will be able to recover quite well.

My sleep is one of the main things that has been affected. Most nights I'll lie awake until four or five in the morning going over everything in my head. When I do sleep I suffer from terrible nightmares. I live on quite a busy road and I hear police sirens going off all the time, which makes me so jumpy. The last time I went back to stay with my parents my dad said that he could hear me pacing up and down the corridor all night because I was unable to sleep. It makes me sad that my parents have to worry about me so much when I should be having the time of my life.

My relationship with food is still a bit affected as well. As much as sometimes I want to eat, I get this panicky feeling in my stomach that means that I can't swallow food down. It's like feeling permanently sick and I literally have to force myself to eat sometimes as I don't wan't to get ill again.

The main difference between the old me and the new me is that I used to love going out. In fact, it was hard to keep me in. But now I have to think twice about leaving the front door, even during the day, because I get very panicky. I feel so nervous about meeting new people and I always think that people are going to set me up or try and do bad things to me. If people play with their phones around me I immediately go on the defensive and think they're plotting something, when they're probably just picking up a text message. I'm totally and utterly paranoid. I really hope I'll be able to learn to trust people again. At the moment I trust about three people in the entire world, which is a real shame as I know that there are a lot of nice people out there.

I really hope that one day I will be able to get married and have kids. If I can find someone I trust enough to settle down with, I really want those things. I know I'm not going to be the easiest person to pin down and I may not always give the best first impression, but hopefully like Snakehips did, someone will able to be able to see past 'crazy Amy'.

I do feel really proud that I managed to get off the drugs on my own. I've heard people say things like, 'I got off drugs and it's all thanks to my boyfriend.' Then they split up with their boyfriend and they're back on the drugs because they don't think they can do it without them. I think if you do it on your own it makes you a much stronger person.

There isn't a 'happy ever after' ending to my story, but at the end of the day I'm still here and I'm still alive. I've beaten my demons and I've fought to get myself back on my feet. You never know how strong you can be until you really have to fight for something. I can only apologise to people I've hurt in the past. I can't make it better and take anything back, but I can make myself better and promise that I will never go down the same route again.

Sometimes the way that people have made mistakes and fought for what they want can make them who they are. And sometimes beauty can be found in imperfection. I moved to London for the bright lights and the glamour, and to try and escape my past, and it nearly destroyed me. Maybe if I had dealt with the first attack and the abortion at the time things would have been very different, but I tried to bury all my feelings. That's something I will never do again.

I'm not on drugs of any kind now – not even anti-depressants – because I don't want to rely on anything. I want to stand on my own two feet and ride the highs and lows and try and learn how to deal with them. From now on, I'm going to feel every little thing, no matter how much it hurts.

The ironic thing is that people take drugs to have a good time. But looking back over the past few years, I can honestly say that I really don't remember having many good times. But I'm hopeful that there will be plenty ahead of me.